Portraits of Valor
Heroic Jewish Women You Should Know

By
Dr. Yvette Alt Miller

Dedicated to:

Miriam and Sarah Raisel,
the most inspiring Jewish women I know

Introduction

A woman of valor - who can find? Those words, written three thousand years ago by King Solomon, describe the ideal Jewish woman. We recite them on Friday night before Shabbat dinner, and they form part of the Hebrew Bible (Proverbs 31:10-31).

In Hebrew, this valorous woman is known as *eishet chayil.* The English translation lacks some of the power of the original: *chayil* can mean valor; it's also the Hebrew word for a soldier. In the Jewish conception, a valorous woman displays her bravery in ways both large and small. King Solomon described her as a businesswoman: "She is like a merchant's ships; from afar she brings her sustenance." She works tirelessly: "She arises while it is yet night, and gives food to her household and a portion to her maidens." This woman of valor is a property-owner and a saleswoman, buying fields and importing goods. She is also wise and kind, God-fearing and humble. She recognizes the emptiness of physical beauty and focuses on the eternal reward of a life well lived instead. This "woman of valor" transcends gender: she is seen as a symbol for all the Jewish people, and her strengths are the goals to which we all strive.

I've thought of this exemplary *Eishet Chayil* many times through the years. In work as a writer for Jewish magazines and websites, I've interviewed countless phenomenal women and men and researched the stories of heroes of the Jewish people, both well known and obscure. If there is any common thread in the remarkable stories I've come across, it is perhaps a quality found at the end of King Solomon's description: "charm is false and beauty is emptiness - the woman who fears God, she shall be praised." King Solomon describes a woman who rejects the everyday concerns that consume most of us and focuses on a higher goal.

Not all of the women I've profiled here were motivated by a traditional belief in God, but they all held fast to a belief in the timeless, enduring, transcendent Jewish cause. Some of the women in these pages dedicated their lives to building and strengthening their Jewish families and communities, to advocating for a Jewish state, to resisting during the Holocaust and saving Jewish lives. Their stories are extraordinary, yet many did not think of themselves as doing anything heroic with their lives. I've been struck time and again, interviewing and writing about people who've managed to change the world, by their modesty, by the insistence that heroic people have that they did nothing special, that anyone else in their shoes would have done the same.

One difference I've noticed between the women and men who make themselves *chayil* - valorous - and the rest of us is their refusal to ignore problems. "We felt like there was a fire burning and we had to put it out. There was always way more to do than we could possibly do, and we just had to do all we could," Pamela Cohen, who worked tirelessly for decades to help Soviet Jews, explains in this book. Those words could have been said by many of the remarkable women in these pages: where other people around them were content to sit back and accept the status quo, they saw a burning need for change that they could not ignore.

This book profiles over 36 women of valor who insisted on doing what was right, in radically different circumstances. Some of the women in these pages were intensely religious; others were adamantly secular. They lived in vastly different eras. Some were married while still in their teens; some remained single or pursued prestigious careers. Some achieved public adulation and success while others displayed their heroism quietly. Some are well known while others remain in obscurity years after their deaths. Yet they are united only in their Jewish heritage and in their belief in building a better world for the Jewish people. The women in this book all, to some extent, embodied King Solomon's ideal of an active, dynamic woman. They largely rejected the lure of "grace and beauty" and found their life meaning in high-minded causes and idealistic goals.

My original goal was to highlight Jewish women whose stories have been lost to history: I didn't set out to write about the most famous Jewish women in our tradition: our Biblical matriarchs Sarah, Rebecca, Rachel and Leah, from whose example we all continue to learn and grow, and who have been written about in many books and articles elsewhere. My goal was to tell the stories of myriad other, lesser known figures. Yet as I worked on this book, I realized that readers have very different perspectives: Jewish women whose biographies might come as a surprise to one person might be familiar to another. Discussing this project with people from diverse backgrounds, I learned that there was a hunger to know more about even women whose stories have been told widely. While many readers have heard of Gold Meir, for instance, many of the details of her life are little known. This book aims to remedy that, bringing her - and the many other women featured in these pages - to life.

In this book's chapter on Rabbi Akiva's wife, I note that the Talmud says "the daughter's actions are the same as her mother's" (Talmud Ketubot 63a). Our mothers, grandmothers, and other ancestors influence us; their legacies and values continue to guide us today. It's my hope that the valorous women profiled in this book inspire a new generation - women and men - to walk in their footsteps and to live their lives with the intensity and burning passions that they embodied.

Acknowledgements

This book would not have been possible without the support of Rabbi Nechemia Cooprsmith, Editor in Chief of Aish.com, who encouraged me to seek out role models and tell their stories. Several of the chapters in this book had their origins on Aish.com. Rabbi Coopersmith, I'm indebted to your passion to uncover new stories and grateful for your unwavering support and collegiality through the years.

Thank you also Rabbi Dr. Leonard Matanky, and Mrs. Renee Rosenberg, for proofreading this book on top of your already busy schedules, and for sharing your knowledge and ideas about the chapters in this book. It is a privilege to work with and learn from both of you. All errors contained herein are my own.

Thanks to my many friends and colleagues who shared their ideas, opinions, passions and interests with me while I was writing this book. Your suggestions enriched this book at every step.

Finally, thank you to my wonderful husband Jeremy, my children Jacob, Simone, Gideon and Natan, my brother Jonathan, my parents, and my parents-in-law for your steadfast support of this project. Thank you for always being interested and encouraging, and for helping me with innumerable technical glitches and questions. You are everything to me.

Chapters

Machla, Noa, Hogla, Milca, and Tirza, daughters of Zelophehad
13th Century BCE

The Torah's Book of Numbers is aptly named in English: much of this Biblical book is taking up with counting the number of Israelites as they sojourned in the desert after their exodus from Egypt. The Hebrew name of Numbers - *Bamidbar* - means "In the Wilderness" and alludes to another aspect of life at that time. After escaping the clutches of Pharaoh and slavery in Egypt, the early Jews had to quickly build a civil society, finding ways to govern a fractious and rebellious people in the midst of a forbidding wilderness landscape.

Numbers opens some time after the Jews' dramatic escape from Egypt. The euphoria of their miraculous escape has worn off, and the grim realities of trying to survive in a semi-arid wasteland are making people on edge. Moses and his brother Aaron order a census of the twelve Israelite tribes, and, later on, use those counts to construct a vast, square-shaped encampment of hundreds of thousands of people. The Torah describes that only adult men were counted: we know the numbers recorded for fighting-age males; the Israelite women remained virtually invisible, uncounted and unmentioned.

Their encampment was huge. On the eastern side were stationed the tribes of Yehuda, Yissachar and Zevulun, totalling 186,400 adult men. To the west were the tribes of Efraim, Menashe and Binyamin; their population of grown men was 108,100. To the south, the tribes of Reuven, Shimon and Gad comprised 151,450 men. To the north, the tribes of Dan, Asher and Naftali comprised 157,600 men.

Each encampment was designated by a huge flag with their tribal symbol, towering over the temporary dwellings below.

It was a paranoid, discordant period. Promised the Land of Israel to settle in, the Israelites complained to Moses that it might not be habitable, insisting that twelve scouts - one from each tribe - sneak over the border and report what they saw. (Ten of the scouts came back with negative reports, spreading fear and despair as they told their fellow tribespeople that the inhabitants of the Land were like giants and would surely crush the weaker Israelites.)

Later on, hundreds of Israelites rebelled against Moses, seeking to install the distinguished elder Korach as their leader instead. Later still, Israelites turned to the pagan god Baal en masse; in retaliation, God sent a plague that killed 24,000 people in the camp.

In the midst of this turmoil and fear, Moses ordered a new census which would soon be used to apportion each tribe's territory once they were safely within the Land of Israel. The count was conducted by Moses and the high priest Elazar, and once again included only men, identifying the sons and grandsons and great grandsons of each family. That is, until five remarkable women insisted on being included in this pivotal census too.

Machla, Noa, Hogla, Milca, and Tirza were daughters of a man named Zelophehad from the tribe of Menasseh. They had no brothers, no "son of Zelophehad" to be included in Moses' count. In the midst of this public counting, the five sisters stepped out of their camp. It's not too difficult to picture the scene. Public life was entirely male in the camp: the Bible elsewhere describes women spending much time inside their tents. Women's voices are almost entirely absent from the Torah's official record of what took place. Yet Machla, Noa, Hogla, Milca and Tirza left their dwelling. Together, they walked through the large, sprawling base and approached Moses and Aaron, in the center of the Israelites' vast encampment. And here, in the full gaze of all the Israelite leaders, they insisted on being counted too.

"...they stood before Moses, before Elazer the Kohen, and before the leaders and the entire assembly at the entrance to the Tent of Meeting, saying: 'Our father died in the wilderness...and he had no sons. Why should the name of our father be omitted from among his family because he had no son? Give us a possession among our father's brothers' (Numbers 27:2-4)."

The women explained that their father was not among those killed in the divine punishment that followed the rebellion against Moses. (Curiously, the Talmud asserts that their father was executed for some offense - the 1st Century sage Rabbi Akiva said Zelophehad was executed for violating Shabbat - yet in the Talmud, his seemingly shameful cause of death doesn't seem to have diminished his daughters' claim to his inheritance.) A son of Zelophehad would have been promised a homestead in the Land of Israel: Why shouldn't his daughters receive land instead?

Instead of dismissing the sisters out of hand, Moses consulted God about their claim. The result changed the course of Jewish history, allowing women to inherit land (in some cases) and exalting Machla, Noa, Hogla, Milca and Tirza.

The language is stirring: "God said to Moses, saying, 'The daughters of Zelophehad speak properly. You shall surely give them a possession of inheritance among the brothers of their father... And to the Children of Israel you shall speak, saying: If a man will die and he has no son, you shall cause his inheritance to pass over to his daughter... This shall be for the Children of Israel as a decree of justice....'" (Numbers 27:1).

Later on, some tribal elders objected. Elders from the tribes of Menasseh, as well as Joseph, approached Moses and complained that if the five sisters married men from other tribes, following the laws of marital property at the time, their homesteads would become property of their husbands' tribes: "Then their inheritance will be subtracted from the inheritance of our fathers and be added to the inheritance of the tribe into which they will marry..." (Numbers 36:3). After consulting God once more, Moses reported that in order to keep the inheritance of Menasseh intact, the sisters had to marry fellow Menasseh clan members. The five sisters gladly complied.

Machla, Noa, Hogla, Milca, and Tirza are exalted in Jewish tradition. The Talmud notes that "The Sages taught: The daughters of Zelophehad are wise, they are interpreters of verses, and they are righteous (Bava Batra 119b)." While it was possible, of course, for God to convey the laws of female inheritance to Moses without these five remarkable women's intervention, they were so God-fearing and righteous that they merited being the means through which the Divine laws were given. Rashi, the great 12th Century Jewish sage, noted that we can infer from the fact that the Torah sometimes lists the five sisters' names in different orders that each one of these five women was as righteous as the others.

The Midrash Rabba, a Medieval collection of Jewish wisdom, goes further: Machla, Noa, Hogla, Milca, and Tirza were not only righteous in and of themselves, they were emblematic of an entire generation of righteous Jewish women.

Soon after leaving Egypt, the Midrash points out, while Moses was at the top of Mount Sinai receiving the Torah, at the base of the mountain some of the Israelite men - but not the women - built a golden calf to worship. "'Remove the gold rings that are in the ears of your wives,' (they said in Exodus 32:2), but the women were unwilling and protested against their husbands" (Midrash Rabbah 21:10).

Later on, when Israelite men slandered the Land of Israel and insisted on sending spies to check it out, the Israelite women refused to believe the negative report of the spies: "The women, however, were not with them in their council," the Midrash asserts. In this view - which has become a central one in Jewish tradition - the daughters of Zelophehad embodied Jewish women's purity and love of the Land of Israel, in contrast to men. The Midrash concludes its discussion about these five righteous women by noting that the Israelite men "did not want to enter the Land, but the women came forward to ask for an inheritance in the Land."

The Talmud records that Machla, Noa, Hogla, Milca, and Tirza each married late in life, all over the age of forty, yet they all were miraculously able to bear children (Bava Batra 119b). Their late ages when they married is taken as further proof of their wisdom: "That they are righteous can be seen from the fact that they did not rush to marry, but rather waited to marry those fit for them" (Bava Batra 119b).

Relatively few details are provided about the lives of Machla, Noa, Hogla, Milca, and Tirza beyond the single dramatic moment when they stood up for their love of the Land of Israel and demanded their family birthright. Yet in that moment, they embodied the exalted qualities of the Jewish people: a devotion to Israel, a sense of decorum and honor, and a fierce determination to ensure that justice and righteousness prevail.

Devorah
1106 BCE - 1066 BCE

When the Israelites first entered the land of Israel after their exodus from Egypt, over 3,000 years ago, much of the northern portion of the land was inhabited by the Canaanites. Numerous records of Canaanite occupation exist: archeologists believe that the name likely meant a reddish-purple color and derived from dyed cloth the Canaanites made and wore.

The Torah is full of descriptions of Israelites' encounters with this war-like people, as well as several other hostile tribes in the area: as soon as Joshua led the Israelite nation into the Land in the 13th Century BCE, a king of Canaan, Jabin king of Hazor, coordinated an alliance of the local nations to fight the Israelite settlers.

"King" might not be the best term for Jabin: he seems to have led a small community centered on Mount Hazor in northern Israel. He controlled this area with metal chariots, however, and was able to maintain military dominance. The Torah records that when Jabin heard of Israelites entering the area, he brokered an alliance with "the kings who were from the north, in the mountain, and in the plain south of Kinneret (Sea of Galilee)...the Canaanite on the east and on the west; and the Amorite and Hittite and the Perizzite and the Jebusite in the mountain; and the Hivvite at the foothills of (Mount) Hermon…and very many horses and chariots" (Joshua 11:2-4).

Despite this impressive military force, the Israelite army, led by Joshua, was victorious, and laid waste to King Jabin's community on Mount Hazor (Joshua 10). The Israelites settled in the land, but things didn't go smoothly for them.

In the land of Israel, the twelve Israelite tribes scattered, each settling in their own portion of the Land of Israel. Two tribes - Gad and Dan, as well as half the tribe of Manasseh - refused to settle in the land of Israel at all, and remained across the Jordan River, in present-day Jordan. The intense sense of national unity that had ignited the Israelites lapsed. Moreover, there were still Canaanite communities scattered across Israel's north, and Jews began to drift away from their religion, worshiping Canaanite gods instead.

A series of Judges ruled the Israelites: after Joshua's death he was succeeded by Otniel ben Kenaz and Ehud ben Gera; the next ruling Judge was a woman named Devorah. (Perhaps as a sign of her strength and ability to deliver a stinging rebuke, her name means "bee" in Hebrew; her name is also related to the Hebrew word for speech; it's said that Devorah was a gifted orator who could teach and persuade people with ease.)

"Devorah was a prophetess, the wife of Lappidoth; she judged Israel at that time," the Bible describes. "She would sit under the date palm of Devorah, between Ramah and Beth-el on Mount Ephraim, and the Children of Israel would go up to her for judgment" (Judges 4:4-5).

Later Jewish commentators describe her as a wealthy woman. Her husband's name Lappidoth means lights and it's speculated that he made torches for the Jewish shrine in nearby Shilo. The Midrash describes Lappidoth as an unlearned man who was guided by his wife towards a life of righteousness and spent his time supporting her work. Devorah was a radiant person who emanated spiritual light: she encouraged her husband to create torches to spread light and learning, too.

The Midrash asks "What is so special about Devorah that she was chosen as Judge for Israel and prophet at that time?" It describes her as so uniquely wise, serious, and scrupulous in her religious observance that she merited becoming Israel's leader and prophet: "It is because whether Jew or non-Jew, man or woman, slave or maidservant, the Divine Spirit rests upon people - all according to their actions" (Eliyahu Rabba 89).

Devorah ruled at a parlous time for the Israelites. The northern Israelite tribes were harassed and attacked by another Canaanite King Jabin (archeologists believe that Jabin was the name of a 400 year long ruling Canaanite dynasty) and his fearsome general, Sisera. Canaanites still maintained a military advantage with their chariots: "The children of Israel cried out to God, for (Sisera) had nine hundred iron chariots, and he oppressed the Children of Israel forcefully for twenty years" (Judges 4:3). It was impossible for Jews to travel on main routes in the north; they had to navigate treacherous mountain trails instead.

The Bible describes Devorah deciding to vanquish Sisera and the Jabin ruler. She called for Barak (some Jewish commentators speculate that Barak - meaning lightning - was another name for Lappidoth) and charged him with leading an attack. Barak insisted that Devorah go with him to battle and she agreed: "God will have delivered Sisera into the hands of a woman," she told him: any victory would be due to her, not to Barak and the army he led.

Devorah and Barak raised 10,000 soldiers from the northern Israelite tribes of Zebulun and Naftali. (He was aided by a local tribe headed by Heber the Kenite, whom the Bible describes as descended from the family of Moses' father-in-law Yitro in Midian, present-day Ethiopia.) They squared off against Sisera's 900 iron chariots.

Israeli President Chaim Herzog has written about Devorah's attack plan in personal terms: he compared Devorah to Israeli Prime Minister Golda Meir, Barak to Israeli Defense Minister Moshe Dayan, and the Israelites' war against Jabin and Sisera to the Yom Kippur War of 1973. He analyzed Devorah's strategy as a contemporary military strategist facing many of the same challenges that she battled 3,000 years ago might do. "Devorah ordered Barak to mobilize 10,000 men and station himself atop Mount Tabor," President Herzog described; "Her own role was to draw Sisera, the commander of King Jabin's forces, towards the valley of the River Kishon to the west, giving Barak the chance to attack from the rear."

President Herzog described the three phases of Devorah's battle plan, and speaks of the advantages of her military positions in modern-day terms. Mount Tabor is "a looming, bulbous mountain which towers over the Jezreel Valley. Its steep sides were a sure defense against the chariots of the enemy. It was also a superb look-out post, with excellent visibility in all directions and an obvious base for a sudden attack on an enemy below."

During the pitched sword battle that ensued, Sisera abandoned his chariot and his army and fled on foot. President Herzog noted that "Sisera's chariots were obviously bogged down in the swampy land of the valley."

Devorah and Barak vanquished the Canaanite forces, and Sisera's end came at the hands of another woman. The Torah describes Sisera running away from battle into territories controlled by Heber the Kenite. He didn't realize that Heber had allied himself with the Israelites, and asked to rest in one of their tents.

Yael, Heber's wife, invited Sisera in. When he demanded water she fed him milk. When he insisted that she keep his whereabouts secret and tell any passing man that nobody was inside her tent, she agreed. She covered Sisera with a blanket and he fell asleep. "Yael...took a tent peg, placed a hammer in her hand, came to him stealthily, and drove the peg into his temple and it went through into the ground (while) he was sleeping deeply and exhausted, and he died" (Judges 4:22).

With the Israelites victorious, Devorah and Barak sang a paean of praise to God known as the Song of Devorah. Generations of Jewish scholars have interpreted this as a divinely-inspired song that represented a new start for the Jewish people as they rejected Canaan's idolatrous ways.

"Hear, oh kings, give ear, oh princes! I, to God shall I sing; I shall sing praise to God, the God of Israel," she sang (Judges 5)

Much of Devorah's Song is devoted to praising the Israelite tribes who joined her battle - and to lamenting the tribes who failed to heed her call. The Israelite tribes of Efraim, Benjamin, Yissachar, Zevulun and Naftali fought together. "Zevulun is

15

a people that risked its life to the death, and so did Naftalie, on the heights of the battlefield," Devorah sang.

Other tribes showed a shocking reluctance to join in Israel's national struggle. "Why did you remain sitting at the borders to hear the bleatings of the flocks?" she asks sarcastically of the other tribes; "The indecision of (the tribe of) Reuven demands great investigation," she sang. (Judges 5:16).

The Bible records that "the land was tranquil for forty years" under Devorah's leadership. Little is known about the remainder of Devorah's life. Recent archaeological discoveries have filled in our knowledge somewhat.

The royal dynasty of Jabin is described not only in the Bible, but elsewhere in ancient records. The Amama Letters, a horde of hundreds of cuneiform-inscribed clay tablets dating from the 14th Century BCE, found in Egypt, refer to the kings named Jabin. They're also mentioned in the Mari Texts, a trove of royal correspondence found along the banks of the Euphrates River in Syria, dating from the 18th Century BCE.

Mount Hazor, the site of the battle, is Israel's largest archeological site. Two layers of burnt ash have been found, corresponding to the Bible's dating of the attacks on Canaan by Joshua and later by Devorah. Devorah's deeds live on, buried in layers of ash on Mount Hazor, as well as in Jewish tradition, where her deeds and the Song of Devorah continue to inspire generations to follow in her example of piety, wisdom and bravery.

Queen Salome Alexandra
141 - 67 BCE

The story of Hanukkah is one of the best-known in Jewish history: how a small group of faithful Jews, led by the Maccabees, revolted against their Hellenist Greek rulers during the years 167-160 BCE, and restored the Temple in Jerusalem to Jewish worship once again. Both their unlikely military victory, and the miracle of a single jug of oil burning in the Temple's grand golden Menorah for eight days, are celebrated in the holiday of Hanukkah. Less known is what came next: The "Maccabee" brothers (named after one brother, Judas Maccabeus) established the Hasmonean royal dynasty that ruled the Jewish kingdom of Judea for over 200 years. Far from presiding over a peaceful nation, the Hasmonean rulers were mercurial, autocratic, and ruled a land continually on the brink of civil war. It fell to Queen Salome Alexandra - also known as Shlomit Alexandra and as Shlomzion - to stand up to some of the most terrifying dictators imaginable, champion traditional Judaism, and restore peace to Judea.

A key fact that's often ignored in telling the Hanukkah story is that many Jews at the time embraced a Hellenist lifestyle, worshiping Greek deities and embracing Greek values. Within a generation of the Hanukkah miracle, the Jewish community was again riven into factions, most notably the Sadducees, who rejected the Talmud and many Jewish elements of a traditional Jewish lifestyle and who dominated the ruling classes, and the Pharisees, who clung to Jewish traditions and lifestyles.

Queen Salome was born into a prominent scholarly family and married into royalty. She seemingly possessed incredible courage and sang-froid. Salome's brother was Shimon ben Shetach, one of Judea's most renowned rabbis and a champion of the Pharisee cause. When it became too dangerous for her brother to remain in Judea because of Sadducee persecution, Queen Salome hid him, as well as other rabbinic allies of traditional Judaism.

Salome's first husband, Judah Aristobulus I, was a grandson of Simon the Maccabee, and ascended the throne in 103 BCE. A paranoid leader with delusions of grandeur, Judah Aristobulus imprisoned his brothers and his mother, who starved to death in jail. He declared himself the first King of Israel since the destruction of the First Temple 500 years before (when the Kingdom of Israel was lost), and embarked on wars with Judah's neighbors. At a time of intense conflict between the upper class Sadducees, who controlled the daily worship in the Temple in Jerusalem, and the more pious Pharisees, who had no such power, Judah Aristobulus allied himself with the Sadducees. He must have been a terrifying, mercurial ruler to oppose, yet Queen Salome used her power to alter his will in every way she could. The few historical records we have of her life describe her as standing in staunch opposition to his tyranny.

After Judah Aristobulus' death, Salome married his brother Alexander Jannai, who crowned himself King Jannai and outdid his brother in irrational cruelty. Once again, Salome used her position to alter royal decrees that threatened traditional Judaism.

During the holiday of Sukkot, King Jannai insisted on serving as High Priest in the Temple. When the time came to pour water on the Temple altar, he shocked the populace by pouring the water on his own feet instead, seemingly implying that he ought to be worshiped. The ensuing outcry sparked a riot that led to widespread civil unrest, pitting traditional Jews against their Sadducee Jewish neighbors. King Jannai took advantage of the turmoil by having most of Israel's rabbinic leaders executed; many of those he failed to kill fled to safety in Egypt. He also disbanded the Sanhedrin, the highest Jewish court, and replaced it with Sadducee judges loyal to him.

Queen Salome used her royal position to reverse these brutal decrees: the Talmud recounts a watershed meal the royal couple ate together. "King Jannai and the Queen ate bread together. And since Jannai executed the Sages, there was no one to recite the Grace after Meals." Queen Salome had a suggestion: "Swear to me that if I bring you such a man, you will not harass him." King Jannai swore, and Queen Salome fetched her own brother, Rabbi Shimon ben Shetach, from hiding (Talmud Berachot 48a).

With her brother restored to his rightful position as a Jewish leader, and with King Jannai often away fighting in foreign wars, Queen Salome did all she could to promote the Pharisee cause, eventually restoring the Sanhedrin itself. Under her reign, Rabbi Shimon, along with Rabbi Joshua ben Gamla, instituted a rule that became a model of Jewish life for thousands of years, mandating that each town and city set up Jewish schools to educate all the local children, teaching poor children for free if they could not afford tuition.

She was opposed at every turn by her husband, who often reversed her popular decrees from afar, but Queen Salome kept trying, legislating traditional Jewish life back into Judean law. Her very name became a testament to her beloved stature: known as Salome Alexandra during much of her life, she gained the popular Hebrew moniker Shlomzion, meaning "Peace of Zion," from her grateful populace.

Queen Salome (now Shlomzion) continued to reign after King Jannai's death in 76 BCE. The nine years she ruled alone were among the most prosperous in ancient Judea's history. She strengthened Israel's military, built fortresses, and oversaw a period of peace and prosperity. The Talmud describes the years of her rule as a time when "rain invariably fell for them on Wednesday eves and on Shabbat eves (times when the Talmud describes people traditionally stayed indoors, so they were not inconvenienced by the showers), until wheat grew as big as kidneys, and barley as big as olive pits, and lentils as golden dinars" (Taanit 23a).

On her deathbed, Salome was torn once more between Judea's internecine fighting. Her son Aristobulus, an ally of the Sadducees, sought the throne. In her final months, she gave into his increasing demands for power - until her last moments, when Salome gave her final instructions: Pharisee leaders should rule Judea after her death, ensuring that traditional Jewish practices would prevail - and preserving Judaism as we know it today for future generations.

Even more important than physical riches, during her reign, God-fearing leadership "restored the Torah to its former glory," the Talmud describes (Kiddushin 66a). That, perhaps more than any other praise, would have pleased Queen Salome, a woman who left scant historical evidence behind, yet who's known and remembered as a staunch and brave defender of traditional Judaism during an intensely chaotic time in Israel's national history.

Queen Helena of Adiabene
First Century CE

In late antiquity, a portion of modern day Iraq formed a small semi-independent kingdom known as Adiabene. The kingdom encompassed the city of Nineveh and was known for its fertile soil and the wealth of its treasuries.

In the first century CE, Adiabene was ruled by a monarch named King Monobaz and his wife Queen Helena. (In various historical records, she is also known as Helene and Hilni.) Jewish traders often passed through the kingdom, and Helena admired their honesty, and enjoyed learning about Judaism for them. One merchant in particular, named Ananias, taught Queen Helena, as well as her son Prince Izates. Both decided to leave the local Ashirite pagan religion and convert to Judaism.

When Queen Helena's husband died, she appointed Izates king. It was the custom at the time for the deceased king's other sons to be put to death in order to ensure that his successor faced no rivals for the throne. Instead of engaging in this barbaric custom, Queen Helena and King Izates were influenced by their new Jewish faith and spared the princes' lives, exiling the dead king's other sons to Rome instead for a time. Eventually, Helena's oldest son, also named Monobaz, returned.

Rabbi Eliezar of Galilee, a scholar from nearby Judea, visited the kingdom, and received a warm welcome from the royal family. Rabbi Eliezar taught Queen Helena and her sons, King Izates and his older brother Prince Monobaz. One day, while reviewing the laws of circumcision, Izates and Monobaz declared their readiness to take this step: with Queen Helena's encouragement, her sons underwent Jewish brit milah (ritual circumcision). The now-Jewish royal family encouraged their subjects to embrace the Jewish faith, as well.

Queen Helena traveled to Jerusalem; the Jewish historian Josephus maintains that she had a magnificent palace built for herself there. During the reign of the Roman Emperor Claudius (41-54 CE), there was a famine in the Land of Israel. Queen Helena used her personal wealth to help alleviate her fellow Jews' suffering, buying grain from Egypt and dried fruits from Cyprus to help feed the populace.

The Talmud mentions Queen Helena several times, always in a tone of gratitude and reverence. At the Jewish holiday of Sukkot, she built a magnificent sukkah in the Judean town of Lod that was twenty cubits high. (At between thirty and forty feet, the Talmud in Sukkah 2b:15-3a:3 describes it as being too tall.) The Talmud also describes a magnificent golden chandelier that she had built for the Temple in Jerusalem. It was placed near the entrance, and each morning as the sun rose it shone on the chandelier and sent rays of brilliant light into the Temple, alerting the priests serving there that dawn had broken and it was time to recite the morning *Shema* (Yoma 37a:17-37b:1).

Other gifts that Queen Helena donated to the Temple include gold handles to be attached to all vessels that were used in the Temple on Yom Kippur, and a magnificent golden plaque on which one of the portions of the Torah was inscribed.

Towards the end of her life, Queen Helena took on the Jewish vows of a Nazir, eschewing wine, not cutting her hair, and not coming into contact with any dead body. Only a commandment that was applicable in Biblical times, the standard length of a Nazirite vow was seven years. The Talmud relates that Queen Helena renewed her vow twice, spending twenty one years in the heightened holy state of being a Nazirite. Much of that time was spent in Jerusalem, where Queen Helena was said to have immersed herself in prayer and good deeds.

Queen Helena outlived her son King Izates. Her son Monobaz ascended the throne and ruled with Queen Helena's continued advice and support. When some of her subjects objected to Queen Helena's generosity in supporting the poor Jews of Judea, King Monobaz II is said to have responded: "My ancestors gathered treasures in this world, while I gather treasures for *Olam HaBa* (The World to Come)."

Helena died in approximately the year 50 CE, probably in Adiabene; King Monobaz II had her remains, as well as those of his brother King Izates, transferred to Jerusalem, where Helena had erected a magnificent tomb. Today, this burial site is known as the Tomb of Kings, and sits within the confines of the City of David, the ancient center of Jerusalem where the high priests and Jewish kings dwelt while the Temple still stood.

The Jewish kingdom of Adiabene lasted until 115 CE, when Roman forces crushed its leaders. Kurdish Jews continue to regard its descendents as part of their Jewish community to this day.

Rachel, Wife of Rabbi Akiva
1st Century CE

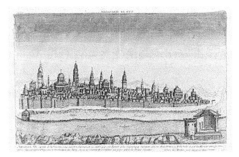

Jerusalem

We catch only glimpses of her, spread across the Talmud's many pages. Her name is thought to be Rachel, and some key details differ in the various tellings of her story. Living in a time when women's existences most often went unrecorded, the life of Rachel, wife of Rabbi Akiva, made a mark, a slight ripple in the historical chronicles which echoes down to our times.

Rabbi Akiva has a greater presence in our history books. Born in about the year 50 CE, he lived through the Roman destruction of Jerusalem in 70 CE. He famously witnessed the heart of Jerusalem, where the Temple had recently stood, silent and ruined and empty. Where a bustling Jewish community so recently had lived, Akiva now observed foxes running wild, unafraid of any humans nearby. Instead of giving into misery and despair, Akiva encouraged his fellow Jews, reminding them that Jewish prophecy promises that a third Temple will one day be rebuilt.

His vivid, poetic words live on after him. He used to describe the good deeds and knowledge that humans accumulate in this world with the powerful metaphor of a person borrowing on credit, and having to pay the Merchant (the Almighty) at the end of his days: "Everything is given on collateral and a net is spread over all the living. The shop is open; the Merchant extends credit...and whoever wishes to borrow, let him come and borrow. The collectors make their rounds constantly, every day, and collect payment from the person whether he realizes it or not..." (Pirkei Avot 3:20).

Standing behind him, in the shadows of history, is his wife. Let's call her Rachel, as tradition dictates. What we do know for certain is the name of her father: ben Kalba Savua. The Talmud describes him as one of the wealthy men of Jerusalem.

Before they were married, Rabbi Akiva's life could not have been more different than the daughter of the great ben Kalba Savua. The Talmud, of which Akiva's is one of the more lively voices, describes young Akiva as an *am ha'aretz*, a man of the land. This variously has meant a humble person, and also an unlearned one. He was employed as the wealthy ben Kalba Savua's shepherd.

Rachel noticed the lowly shepherd, saw his potential, and recognized a kindred spirit. "The daughter of Ben Kalba Savua saw that he was humble and refined. She said to him: If I betroth myself to you, will you go to the study hall to learn Torah?" the Talmud describes. Akiva readily agreed. When he learned of Akiva's and Rachel's secret betrothal, ben Kalba Savua became enraged and took a vow cutting Rachel off entirely.

The newlyweds were left utterly destitute. The Jerusalem Talmud describes Rachel resorting to selling her hair in order to support herself and Akiva. The Babylonian Talmud recounts that "In the winter they would sleep in a storehouse of straw." Each morning, Akiva would tenderly pull loose strands of straw from Rachel's hair. When a poor stranger (whom the Talmud relates was none other than the prophet Elijah in disguise) came to ask if they had any straw to spare for his poor wife, who'd just given birth, Akiva and Rachel shared their meager possessions and counted themselves lucky. "We should be happy with our lot, as we at least have straw to sleep on," the Talmud recounts Akiva saying to his wife (Nedarim 50a).

With Rachel's encouragement, Akiva traveled far away to study with the greatest rabbis of the day. In time, he took on his own students. News of Akiva's fame spread throughout the ancient land of Israel, and in time 12,000 students called Rabbi Akiva their teacher.

All that time, Rachel stayed at home, working and earning enough money for both her and Akiva to survive. Life was terribly hard. After twelve years, Akiva returned home to his wife. The Babylonian Talmud relates what happened next. "As he approached he heard an old man saying to his wife: For how long will you lead the life of a widow of a living man, living alone while your husband is in another place? She said to him: If he would listen to me, he would sit and study for another twelve years" (Ketubot 62b). Akiva heard her words, and turned around to return to his study hall for another twelve years.

Finally, after he'd doubled the number of his students and was arguably the most renown sage in the land, Akiva returned to his wife, bringing his students with him. Rachel ran out to greet her husband. Horrified that such a poor, ragged woman was approaching their revered teacher, some of Akiva's students pushed her away. "Leave her alone!" Akiva cried: ""My Torah knowledge and yours is actually hers!"

With Rabbi Akiva back home in Jerusalem, ben Kalba Savua petitioned to have his vow dissolved, and gave half his money to Rachel and Akiva.

Besides Rachel's selfless devotion to helping her husband become a great Torah scholar, one other distinctive fact has endured through the ages, giving us a sense of what Rachel might have looked like. The Talmud discusses a peculiar type of headdress that wealthy Jewish women living in the land of Israel used to wear in ancient times: a sort of tiara or crown made of cloth or precious metals, that was sculpted to look like a model of a city. Rabbi Akiva gave Rachel a beautiful crown made of gold that was fashioned to look like the city of Jerusalem.

We know little of Rachel's death, though it's clear that her legacy of generosity lived on after her. Akiva was put to death by the Roman authorities who ruled Judea after the unsuccessful Jewish revolt of 132 CE known as the Bar Kochba Rebellion. He's said to have been tortured to death in the Roman amphitheater in the Israeli city of Caesarea. Unrecorded is whether or not the Romans murdered his wife as well.

The Talmud does note that Rachel and Akiva had a daughter. Though her name too is lost to history, their daughter helped another man become a scholar too. "Rabbi Akiva's daughter did the same thing for ben Azzai, who was also a simple person, and she caused him to learn Torah in a similar way, by betrothing herself to him and sending him off to study. This explains the (Ancient Jewish Aramaic) folk saying that people say: "The ewe follows the ewe; the daughter's actions are the same as her mother's" (Talmud Ketubot 63a).

Rachel's legacy also lives on in Rabbi Akiva's words. For after all, his Torah was her Torah, too.

Bruria
2nd Century CE

Page of the Talmud

She lived during one of the most horrific periods of Jewish history, the violent, terrifying years in the aftermath of the Roman destruction of the Jewish Temple in Jerusalem in 70 CE: the Jewish scholar Bruria was a brilliant woman devoted to learning Torah and living a fully Jewish life. One of the few women whose words are recorded in the Talmud, the scattered few times she appears hint at a life full of heartbreak and overshadowed by Roman brutality.

Bruria's father was the great Talmdic sage Rabbi Chanina ben Tradyon; her husband was another well-known Talmudic figure, Rabbi Meir. Yet her family's eminence was no protection at all against the grotesque caprices of the Roman authorities ruling Judea in at the time - and also offered no protection against the strong currents of jealousy and rivalry that eventually tore her family apart.

While Bruria was learning Torah, eventually acquiring the skills that would place her among the Talmud's eminent sages, a Roman noble kidnapped her sister and eventually sold Buria's sister into sexual slavery. "Why was (Rabbi Chanina ben Tradyon's" daughter) condemned to sit in a brothel?" the Talmud asks (Avoda Zara 18a).

The Talmud relates that Bruria rescued her sister, instructing her husband Rabbi Meir to go and free her. "Rabbi Meir went and dressed as a Roman knight" and entered the brothel, posing as a customer. He identified Bruria's sister, who begged him to choose someone else to consort with. "Rabbi Meir went over to the guard, and said to him: Give her to me. The guard said to him: I fear that if I do so, I will be punished by the government. Rabbi Meir said to him: Take this vessel full of dinars; give half to the government as a bribe, and half will be for you…." (Avoda Zara 18a). Rabbi Meir had to show the guard a miracle - carnivorous dogs failed to attack him - to prove that he enjoyed God's favor on this mission, and was finally able to free Bruria's sister.

Of Buria's brothers, we know only that one became a criminal and was eventually murdered by his villainous associates, who killed him by filling his mouth with dust and stones. Another brother, Shimon, was a renown Torah scholar, but Bruria's knowledge and understanding is recorded as exceeding his. (Some say that Shimon was the same brother who later became a thief, driven to a life of degeneracy after his sister Bruria upstaged him.)

Once a man from the town of Kfar Chananiah asked Shimon a point of law concerning the purity status of a kosher oven. Shimon provided an answer, and Bruria disagreed, offering her own interpretation of Jewish law. The siblings apparently got into a furious argument defending their different points of view. "When the argument was relayed in front of the Rabbi Yehudah ben Bava, he said '(Rabbi Chanina ben Tradyon's) daughter (Bruria) spoke better than his son (Shimon)." (Tosefta Keilim Kamma 4:9)

Bruria's rulings and opinions related to Jewish law live on in the Talmud. Her words echo through the ages, at times giving us a glimpse of her quick mind and sardonic sense of humor. In one memorable passage, Rabbi Yosei HaGelili is walking along a pathway when he meets Bruria. "Which road goes to Lod?" he asked her, using a simple Hebrew sentence containing four words (*B'ezeh derech l'lech b'Lod?*). Instead of answering, Bruria chided him (and possibly the mores of the time which discouraged men from talking with women). "Foolish Galilean, didn't the Sages say: Do not talk much with women? You should have said your question more succinctly: "Which way to Lod?" (*B'ezeh l'Lod?*), Bruria answered him, providing a way to phrase his question that shaved off two words from his original inquiry (Eruvin 53b: 24-25a:1).

Bruria's world was brutal and filled with bandits and other criminals. The Talmud relates "There were...hooligans in Rabbi Meir's neighborhood who caused him a great deal of anguish" (Berachot 10a:2-4). Rabbi Meir prayed for these criminals' deaths, but Bruria contradicted him. "What is your thinking? On what basis do you pray for the death of these hooligans?" Invoking Psalm 104, which calls on God to "let sins cease from the land," Bruria noted a distinction: the Psalm states that sins, not sinners, should be erased. "Rather, pray for God to have mercy on (sinners), that they should repent, for if they repent, then the wicked will be no more...." Bruria urged. Her words swayed her husband, who did pray for the local ruffians, who later repented.

One of the best known stories of Bruria is also one of the most tragic. The Midrash describes Bruria as the embodiment of King Solomon's Woman of Valor whom he described in Proverbs 31:10. As proof, the Midrash describes a heartbreaking scene.

"There was a story about Rabbi Meir who was sitting and expounding in the study hall on Shabbat afternoon, when two of his sons died. What did his mother do? She placed both of them on the bed and spread a sheet over them." Bruria waited until Rabbi Meir returned home after Shabbat and asked him if she could pose a question of Jewish law: "Before today, a man came and deposited something with me, and now he is coming to take it. Should we return it to him or not?"

Rabbi Meir answered that of course Bruria had to return the deposit. "She grabbed his hand, brought him up to that room, had him approach the bed and took off the sheet from upon them." Rabbi Meir was overwhelmed with grief, and Bruria somehow found words to comfort him. "Is this not what I told you? Do I not need to return the deposit to its Owner?" Bruria asked. Her words eased her husband's heart: "The Lord has given and the Lord has taken; may the name of the Lord be blessed (Job 1:21)," Rabbi Meir replied (Midrash Mishlei 31:2).

Bruria's life contained yet more horrific tragedy. Romans arrested her father Rabbi Chanina ben Tradyon for teaching Torah and publicly burned him alive. (The Midrash relates that they also murdered Bruria's mother.) Bruria's husband Rabbi Meir was a wanted man, subject to arrest for the crime of teaching Torah: Roman authorities "went and engraved the image of Rabbi Meir at the entrance of Rome where it would be seen by everyone, and they said: Anyone who sees a man with this face should bring him here." (Avoda Zara 18b). Rabbi Meir escaped, the Talmud relates, by using one of three ruses: two involved seeming to consort with prostitutes and one included appearing to eat non-kosher food. Since the Romans understood that the esteemed Rabbi Meir would do none of these un-Jewish acts, his scheme allowed him to escape arrest.

Immediately after this, the Talmud describes, "Rabbi Meir arose, fled, and arrived in Babylonia." History is unclear about the exact reason for his flight: "There are those who say that he fled because of this incident (in which he evaded arrest), and there are those who say that he fled due to embarrassment from the incident involving his wife Bruria (Avoda Zara 18b.) The Talmud is silent on what this incident might have been, but a millennium later, an answer was provided in the name of the Medieval Jewish sage Rashi, who wrote a commentary on the Torah and Talmud, laying a grave charge against both Rabbi Meir and Bruria, and marring her reputation forever.

There's a great deal of dispute over whether the description of Bruria's end truly was written by Rashi. In this description often attributed to Rashi, Bruria mocked Jewish sages who described women as weak. The commentary describes Rabbi Meir hearing this and deciding to prove his wife wrong by asking one of his students to seduce Bruria, thereby showing that she didn't have the fortitude to resist. After pestering Bruria repeatedly, the commentary describes, the student eventually succeeded in seducing Bruria. Overwhelmed by remorse, Bruria supposedly ended her own life by strangling herself. "And Rabbi Meir ran away due to embarrassment," this commentary concludes (Rashi on Avoda Zara 18b).

Bruria has been trailed by this story for a thousand years, marking her as a flawed and fallen woman. (The commentary has also marred the reputation of its supposed author Rashi.) Yet Bruria's brilliance and commitment to Torah can never be forgotten. A more fitting legacy for this brilliant woman is found in the Talmud's volume Pesachim (62b: 8-9): "Bruria, wife of Rabbi Meir and daughter of Rabbi Chanina ben Tradyon, was so sharp and had such a good memory that she learned three hundred *halachot* (Jewish laws) in one day from three hundred Sages." A rare, vivid, luminous woman, Bruria lived through horrors we cannot imagine. Her legacy is a complex and inspiring one.

Pulcelina
died 1171

Auto-da-fe (Burning at the Stake)

Their names are largely forgotten, though scholars have long documented their existence: In the Middle Ages, Jewish women worked throughout Europe as traders and money lenders, often supporting their families while their husbands were away for long periods on commercial trips. Over half of the Jews working as money lenders in France at this time were widows.

In numerous accounts from the eleventh through thirteenth centuries, "women are shown leaving their homes without any restrictions or suspicion and as playing an important role in the support of the family," records Israeli historian Avraham Grossman. Their freedoms of movement and dress often exceeded those of their female Christian neighbors, who were discouraged from doing business or even going out of doors. With Christians forbidden to lend money by the Catholic Church, Jews - often Jewish women - stepped in to provide this vital service. One nearly forgotten woman who lived in the French city of Blois was a widow named Pulcelina; she lived with her two daughters and worked as a money lender.

Avraham Grossman provides a mention of a Jewish woman who lived in eleventh century Germany, during the First Crusade, as an example of a typical Jewish businesswoman at the time: "There was an important woman *(isha hashuvah)* whose name was Minna...and they did not wish to kill her, for her name was known far and near, for all the great ones of her city and the princes of the land used her services" as a money lender, a Medieval letter records. Her business acumen and wealth - like that of other Jewish money lenders, including Pulcelina - rendered them "important" with weighty roles in their communities and positions commanding respect.

By far, most surviving references to prominent women of the era are just scraps: with so few historical records documenting the lives of ordinary Jews, it is hard to piece together the lives of women and men in that era. One exception is Pulcelina. Her influence, her bravery, her piousness and her fame live on thanks to five contemporary letters, as well as a historical account of her death written by the great Jewish sage Rabbi Ephraim ben Jacob.

Life for Pulcelina and other Jews in northern France at the time, as in much of Europe, was precarious. The First Crusade, sparked in 1096 when Pope Urban II called on Christians to liberate the Holy Land, led to devastating massacres of Jews in Northern Europe. The Second Crusade was declared in 1147.

Added to these tragedies which whipped up anti-Jewish hatred was the emergence of blood libels. In 1144 Jews in the English city of Norwich were accused of murdering a young boy as part of their celebration of Passover. Similar accusations were made against Jews in the English town of Gloucester in 1168. This vile charge that Jews murdered Christian children as part of their holiday celebrations leapt the English Channel and surfaced in the town of Blois, Pulcelina's home in northern France, in 1771.

Theobald V, Count of Blois, was closely linked to Pulcelina, probably by being far in her debt (as many monarchs relied on Jews to finance their armies and their lifestyles). A contemporary letter describes her as a powerful woman, acting arrogantly to others "with the Count's sanction." The letter also describes her as dealing "harshly" with people in business, including Ajix, the Count's wife. The letter uses the Hebrew word *ohav*, love or like, to describe the Count's feelings towards Pulcelina.

The historian Susan Einbinder believes that the Count was Pulcelina's patron. Some modern historians have assumed that Pulcelina was either a literary invention or a harlot who slept with the Count. Contemporaneous accounts of her life, however, describes her as a God-fearing money lender who'd extended a large line of credit to Theobald V and many other aristocrats in the region.

....In the year 4931 (1171), evil appeared in France...and great destruction in the city of Blois, in which at that time there lived about forty Jews....

So recorded Rabbi Ephraim ben Jacob (1133-1198), one of the Tosafists, a prominent group of Jewish religious scholars who commented on the Talmud in the Middle Ages and whose work is still read today. Rabbi Ephraim ben Jacob was also a poet, and wrote many Hebrew language prayers and poems. His book *Sefer Zechira*, Book of Remembering, details several massacres of Jews across northern Germany and France, some of which he himself only narrowly escaped. By his own account, he knew Pulcelina and other Jews from Blois, as well as Jews from neighboring towns who witnessed what occurred there.

One day, a local soldier stopped in the gloom of evening at a river to water his horse. In the near-dark, the soldier spied a local Jew by the name of Isaac bar Eleazar, who was also watering his horse. Isaac was wearing a tunic of untanned animal hide, and in the gathering evening, it looked to the frightened soldier like the carcass of a child. The soldier concocted a story that Isaac had been holding a Christian child and had thrown him into the water. Rabbi Ephraim records:

The soldier knew that his master would rejoice at the fall of the Jews, because he hated a certain Jewess, influential in the city. He as much as put the following words into his master's mouth: 'Now I can wreak my vengeance on that person, on the woman Pulcelina.

After the soldier delivered his deceitful report, his master rode into Blois to tell Count Theobald what the local Jews had supposedly done. Theobald "became enraged" and had all the Jews of Blois placed in chains in a dank prison: forty Jews in total. The sole exception was Pulcelina, whom he ordered not to be chained up.

Perhaps sensing that she could prevail on Theobald to show the Jews mercy, Pulcelina remained calm, encouraging her fellow Jews that she might sway the Count. Her two daughters were among the Jews imprisoned in the jail; the pressure to appear cheerful and optimistic must have been enormous. Count Theobald was already entering negotiations with neighboring Jewish communities to settle a ransom for the Jews of Blois, and it must have seemed that within days the Jews of Blois would be freed from their hellish jail. Rabbi Ephraim described the scene thus:

....But Dame Pulcelina encouraged them all, for she trusted in the affection of the ruler who up to now had been very attached to her....

Tragically, according to Rabbi Ephraim, Pulcelina underestimated Theobald V's wife, Alix of France, a daughter of King Louis VII of France and Eleanor of Aquitaine. She hated Pulcelina and ordered the guards not to let her speak with Count Theobald. (Some historians believe even this detail was invented as a way to inject romance into Pulcelina's tale and depict her as a romantic heroine instead of a capable businesswoman whose esteem stemmed from her business activities and acumen.)

Instead of negotiating with local Jews, Theobald began hearing from a fanatically anti-Jewish local Augustinian priest, who inserted himself in the talks, harangued Count Theobald to abandon his plans to accept a ransom in exchange for the Jews of Blois, and escalated anti-Jewish feelings in the town. Nine Jews were indeed ransomed, but 31 were condemned to be burned at the stake. Most of the condemned Jews were women, and Pulcelina and her daughters were included in their number. Rabbi Ephraim wrote what happened next:

....In the meantime the priest arrived on the scene, and from this time on the ruler paid no attention to the Jews and did not listen to them, but only to the instructions of the priest. In the day of wrath money could not help them. At the wicked ruler's command they were taken and put into a wooden house around which were placed thorn bushes and faggots. As they were led they were told: 'Save your lives. Leave your religion and turn to us.' They mistreated them, beat them, and tortured them, hoping that they would exchange their glorious religion...but they refused.

Rather did they encourage each other and say to one another: 'Persist in the religion of the Almighty!'

Contemporary Christian accounts maintain that some Jews did convert, but Pulcelina and her daughters are not recorded among them. Two rabbis from the group were burned first, tied to a stake that was set alight. When the flames broke the bonds that held them, the rabbis tried to escape, saying that they had survived the Christians' trial of fire and now deserved to live, but they were beaten back by the mob, who killed them with swords and threw their bodies into the flames.

All together, thirty-one Jews were killed, including Pulcelina, who just days before had tried to give hope to her fellow Jews, including her two daughters. Jews from the nearby city of Orleans, who had tried in vain to ransom their coreligionists, were present at the burning, and later wrote that as they died, the Jews of Blois "sang in unison a melody that began softly but ended with a full voice." The prayer was the *Aleinu*, sung in synagogues around the world every day; the tune that the Jews of Blois sang in their final moments was the haunting melody used to this day in many Ashkenazi synagogues on Rosh Hashanah.

The few surviving Jews of Blois negotiated with Theobald for the right to bury the victims. They also called for an annual fast to commemorate their deaths, though this never was widely adopted.

Little is remembered of Pulcelina beyond her death; even less is recorded of the thirty Jews with whom she died, including her children, friends and relatives. *Oh daughters of Israel, weep for the thirty-one souls that were burnt for the sanctification of the Name, and let your brothers, the entire house of Israel, bewail the burning*, Rabbi Ephraim recorded. His piercing words are as true today as a thousand years ago.

Sadly, Pulcelina's reputation was soon tarnished for future generations. A century later, Rabbi Meir of Rothenburg (1215-1293) wrote his own account of the murder of the Jews of Blois, in which he cast Pulcelina as a villain and a harlot. The 16th Century French Jewish historian Yosef HaCohen altered Pulcelina's memory further, depicting her as a tragic martyr who would never have engaged in anything as base as business or money lending. It's a more sympathetic account than Rabbi Meir's, but it changes her memory beyond recognition, using Pulcelina and her tragic story as a vehicle for describing his own times' view of ideal womanhood. A 1927 play *Pulzelinah*, by the Hebrew scholar Shlomo Dov Goitein, portrayed Pulcelina as a pious businesswoman, but also dwelt heavily on her supposedly romantic allure to men.

She deserves better. Though few facts about Pulcelina survive, we know her name, her town, her profession as money lender and businesswoman, and can recognize the high esteem in which she was held by Jews and Gentiles alike. We also know the manner of her horrific murder, and the brave way she and her fellow Jews met their death. For these reasons alone, Pulcelina deserves our recognition and our esteem. May her memory - and the memory of the 31 Jews of Blois with whom she was murdered - be a blessing to us all.

Dulcea of Worms
Died 1191

Following the devastation of the First Crusade of 1096, the Jews of Worms, a town in northern Germany, rebuilt a flourishing community. Boasting at least two synagogues (one for men and an adjacent one devoted to women), a mikvah, a community center, a wedding hall and a Jewish hospital, Worms soon became one of the region's most important Jewish centers. In the late 1100s, a synod of Jewish leaders from the towns of Worms, Mainz and Speyer took control of guiding Jewish communities throughout the Germanic lands of northern Europe.

In Mainz, a small group of highly educated, intellectually-inclined Jews studied and penned Jewish texts: they were dubbed the *Hasdei Ashkenaz*, the Pious ones of Germanic Lands. Prominent among these scholars were a revered and wealthy couple, Rabbi Eliezar ben Judah of Worms (1165-1230) - sometimes known as the *Rokeach*, or "Perfumer", after the title of his best-known book - and his distinguished wife, Dulcea.

The family lived in comfort with their two daughters, Bellette and Hannah and a son named Jacob. At any given time, students were likely to be lodging in their home as well. Like many Medieval Jewish women, Dulcea supported her family through money lending. It was her material success, historians believe, that might have led to her eventual tragic death.

As well as undertaking business enterprises, Dulcea was an accomplished craftswoman and embroiderer. She joined books and sewed pieces of vellum together to create forty Torah scrolls, a massive undertaking. She was also a matchmaker and helped Jewish brides prepare for their weddings, and performed *tahara*, bathing the dead and preparing the deceased for burial.

What little we know of Dulcea today comes from a poem that Rabbi Eliezar wrote about her after her death: he goes through the lines of the Jewish song "A Woman of Valor" (Proverbs 31), in which King Solomon describes the ideal Jewish woman. After each sentence, Rabbi Eliezar adds a personal comment about how Dulcea embodied each of the song's ideal traits.

According to her husband, Dulcea was known for her good deeds. Her business acumen allowed the family to purchase books. "Vigorous in everything, she spun threads for phylacteries, and (prepared) sinews (to bind together) scrolls and books; she was as swift as a deer to cook for the young men and to fulfill the needs of the students…. She prepared meat for special feasts and set her table for all of the community." Rabbi Eliezar describes Dulcea as learned and pious: "In all the cities she taught women… She knew the order of morning and evening prayer; she came early to the synagogue and stayed late… She was eager, pious, and amiable in fulfilling all the commandments," he wrote.

One night, on the 22nd of the Hebrew month of Kislev in the Jewish year of 4959 - November 22, 1196 in the Common Era - disaster struck. Two armed men broke into the family home, likely determined to rob Dulcea because of her well-known wealth. In a separate poem about his daughter Bellette, who was 13 years old, and Hannah, who was six, Rabbi Eliezar described what happened next: "Two despicable ones came and killed them before my eyes and wounded me and my students and also my son."

Elsewhere, Rabbi Eliezar described the horrific events of that night more fully, and how Dulcea saved her husband at the cost of her own life. It was evening, and Rabbi Eliezar had just finished talking about the weekly Parsha. It's likely that Dulcea enjoyed her husband's words of Torah, the last she ever heard. "I was

40

sitting at my table (and) two...men came to us, and they drew their swords and struck my pious wife, mistress Doce. They broke the head of my elder daughter Bellette, and they struck my younger daughter Hannah in the head, and they both died."

The swordsmen next struck Jacob, causing a huge gash on his head from his forehead to his chin. They turned their swords on Rabbi Eliezar and wounded him in the head and hand, and also attacked some students and an assistant teacher who were in the house. "Immediately, the pious woman (Dulcea) jumped up and ran out of the winter quarters and cried out that they were killing us."

As she ran through the town screaming, the swordsmen chased after Dulcea, slashing her violently until she fell dead. That gave Rabbi Eliezar the chance to bolt his door and shout for help, which swiftly came. "And I cried out over this pious woman, praying for revenge," he described, his anguish still ringing through his prose today.

Local authorities soon caught and executed the murderers, but Rabbi Eliezar's sorrow and guilt could never be assuaged: he blamed himself, for if Dulcea hadn't supported him through her money lending business, she might never have become a target of the murderous thugs who killed her and her daughters.

His lasting call to avenge Dulcea's death has served as her epitaph through the centuries: "May the Holy One show us their revenge and take pity on their souls, and may he have compassion for the survivor who remains, and on my son, and on his people Israel... May her soul be bound in the wrappings of eternal life...."

Licoricia of Winchester
died 1277

Statue of Licoricia of Winchester in Winchester, England

(Courtesy of William Carver)

Britain's newest statue was unveiled on February 10, 2022 in the town of Winchester. "We recall…there was an extraordinary lady committed to her faith who was determined to raise her family, build a successful enterprise and give a contribution of inestimable value to her country," Chief Rabbi Ephraim Mirvis told the large crowd assembled to see the statue.

The woman who was being honored, Licoricia of Winchester, was renowned in her day. Though she was largely forgotten until recently, in the 1200s, Licoricia was one of the wealthiest and most prominent women in all of England. She rubbed shoulders with royalty and occupied a place of prestige and importance in King Henry III's court. When she died, news of her passing reached far and wide, far beyond England's shores.

Little is known of Licoricia's early life. She was born in the early 1200s and married a man named Abraham, son of Isaac. Abraham seems to have originated in Kent, and moved to Winchester, where there was a small Jewish community. There, he and Licoricia had three sons, Isaac (whose English name was Cokerel), Baruch (Benedict) and Lumbard; and a daughter named Belia.

In the 1200s, Jews lived in England under the protection of the king, and were considered the private "property" of the monarch. Jews were barred from most professions, were forbidden from owning land, and were largely forced into money lending. When an English Jew died, their property and assets couldn't be inherited by their children: all wealth was claimed by the Crown. Beginning in 1194, King Richard I restricted Jews' money lending activity: Jews were forced to conduct all money lending business in just a few official locations: historian Richard Huscroft identified "six or seven" locales in all of England where Jews could legally conduct business. The towns of London, Norwich, Lincoln, and Winchester were among the first places so designated; several more later joined the list.

Estimates of the number of Jews living in England vary widely, but it's likely that the Jewish community in Winchester numbered no more than eighty people at the time Licoricia lived there. Most Jews lived clustered together in a central avenue called Jewry street. They were a close-knit group who supported and helped one another. Women, as well as men, worked in business, and some women formed business partnerships.

Life was incredibly hard for England's Jews at the time. The first instance of a blood libel - where Jews were accused of killing a Christian child in order to use his blood in Jewish rituals - occurred in 1144 in the English town of Norwich. A second blood libel took place in 1255 - during Licoricia's lifetime - when the body of a young child was found in a well in the town of Lincoln. The boy's friends accused local Jews of kidnapping, torturing and murdering the child. Lincoln's sheriff arrested over 90 Jews; 18 were executed. Both of the children at the centers of these blood libels were made into saints (St. William of Norwich and St. Hugh of Lincoln), stoking Christian hatred of local Jews still further.

In 1239, King Henry III ordered all of England's Jews to turn over a third of their belongings and assets to the crown; Jews who couldn't pay were imprisoned in the Tower of London while their property was seized. In 1253, all Jews in England were forced to wear a piece of cloth or parchment in the shape of two stone tablets on their clothes, representing the stone tablets that Moses brought down from Mount Sinai. Wealthy Jews could pay to avoid wearing this mark. (Historians speculate that Licoricia was among those Jews who avoided wearing the degrading garment.)

In 1265, during the unsuccessful rebellion of Simon de Montfort against the king, fighting came to Winchester as King Henry III's soldiers routed the rebellion. In the violence, many Christians in Winchester turned on their Jewish neighbors, attacking Winchester's Jews and seizing their property. Terrified Jews managed to find refuge inside Winchester Castle; many of those who couldn't make it into the fortress in time were murdered. When the siege ended, the traumatized survivors left the fortress and picked up the pieces of their lives, somehow resuming business and communal life. Winchester's Jews rebuilt their lives amid neighbors who helped murder their friends and family.

It was against this turbulent and terrifying backdrop that Licoricia built her money lending business, eventually becoming one of the wealthiest women in all of England.

The first historical documents that mention her date from early 1234, after the death of her husband Abraham. Licoricia remained in Winchester with her children after his death and continued in the family business of money lending, going into business with another Jewish woman living in Winchester named Belia.

At some point Licoricia became acquainted with another Jewish money lender, David of Oxford, who was one of the wealthiest Jews living in England. A communal leader, King Henry III used David to help him enforce his onerous taxes and regulations on England's Jews. In the early 1240s, David was married to a woman named Muriel, who helped him in his business: when he met Licoricia, however, David decided to divorce Muriel and seek Licoricia's hand in marriage.

The divorce wasn't easy to obtain: Muriel refused to accept it. Two hundred years before, Rabbi Gershom of Mainz had ruled that a Jewish divorce could only be valid when both parties agreed. Muriel insisted that a Beit Din, a rabbinical court, hear her side and adjudicate in her marriage. As was the custom among English Jews at the time, Muriel and her family convened a Beit Din in France, where there was a larger and more scholarly Jewish community. The Beit Din ruled in Muriel's favor, and a second Beit Din in Oxford threw out the divorce.

However, David was determined to obtain his divorce, and turned to King Henry III for help. King Henry III eagerly seized this chance to revoke the Jews' autonomy in their civil and religious matters, and ordered his religious leaders to uphold the divorce, which they did. David set up a new house and allowance for Muriel, as Jewish law mandated he do after the divorce, and Licoricia and David soon married.

Licoricia had a child with David, a son named Asher (known in English variously as Asser, Sweteman or Sweetman), but her marriage to David was short lived: David died in 1244, after only two years of marriage. Upon his death, all of his business records were taken to London to the *Scaccarium Judaeorum*, the special court in which Jewish business dealings were scrutinized and regulated. Licoricia was immediately looked at with suspicion: while the business was being assessed, in order to prevent Licoricia from interfering in any way, authorities arrested Licoricia and imprisoned her in the Tower of London.

The Tower was a fearsome prison for English Jews: it is where the 90 Jews from Lincoln had been taken after being accused of ritual murder, and was the site of the execution of 18 of them. Yet the Tower had also served as a refuge to local Jews during violent anti-Jewish pogroms: A number of Jews were murdered during King Richard I's coronation in 1189, so before his coronation in 1216, King Henry III took steps to protect local Jews, allowing them to take shelter in the Tower of London.

There are records of Jewish prisoners in the Tower of London paying their jailors to obtain kosher food, and of Jewish prisoners paying bribes to be allowed to observe Yom Kippur in the prison. It's possible that Licoricia engaged in similar bribery during her imprisonment there, while David's business affairs were settled.

After several months, David's business records were finally released and Licoricia went free. She was offered the chance to buy back David's outstanding loans at the exorbitant price of 5,000 marks. Licoricia somehow raised the money and went into business for herself. (In a particularly insulting gesture, most of her fee went to a special fund to build a new shrine to Edward the Confessor in Westminster Abbey.)

Licoricia took her children and returned to Winchester to start a new chapter in her life. There, she built up an even larger money lending business. She lent funds directly to King Henry III, and visited his court whenever he visited Winchester. She also lent money to members of his royal court, to Queen Eleanor, and to local business people and farmers as well. She likely was outgoing and gregarious, with a winsome personality that drew people of all social classes to her and engendered trust. Legal records at the time record Licoricia's business dealings across a wide swath of southern England over the next thirty years, usually in partnership with her sons. She lent to rich and poor alike, and also extended credit to her fellow Jews, helping support businesses. In time Licoricia became an intermediary between the Jewish community and the crown.

In 1258, Licoricia's close business relations with King Henry III led to her being imprisoned in the Tower of London for a second time. Belia, the woman who had worked with Licoricia as a business partner years before, wished to give a gold ring to King Henry III, perhaps as a bribe or to curry favor with the monarch. She entrusted it with her good friend Licoricia to deliver, but disaster struck. The ring disappeared and one of Licoricia's neighbors, a woman named Ivetta, accused Licoricia of taking it. Once more, the authorities threw Licoricia into the Tower of London while the matter was investigated: Ivetta was eventually determined to be the thief, and King Henry III ordered Licoricia to be released. (The ring was never found.)

After a long and successful business career, disaster struck.

One day in 1277, Licoricia's daughter Belia went to visit her mother and was confronted by a horrific sight: Licoricia and her Christian maid, a woman known as Alice of Bicton, lay dead in the house, both stabbed to death. A large amount of money was gone, presumably stolen by the murderer or murderers. Local authorities identified three men as possible culprits and brought them to trial, but a jury acquitted all three. (Conveniently, they named a man who'd left the city and who couldn't be traced as the prime suspect.) Licoricia's sons Cokerel and Sweteman later tried to bring another case against the three men who likely murdered their mother, but with the legal system stacked against Jews, they were unsuccessful. News of Licoricia's death spread far and wide throughout the Jewish world, reaching communities as far afield as France and Germany, where she was mourned.

The thirteen years following Licoricia's death were crushing for England's Jewish community.

When King Henry III died in 1272, King Edward I ascended the throne and faced increasing pressure from indebted aristocrats to end Jewish money lending. In 1287, he ordered England's Jews to pay an enormous tax of 20,000 marks to the crown: in Winchester, the entire Jewish community was imprisoned in Winchester Castle until the onerous tax was raised. Licoricia's youngest son, Asher, was amongst them. While imprisoned, he carved a message in Hebrew into his prison cell's wall: "On Friday Eve of the Sabbath in which the Parsha Emor is read, all Jews of the land of the isle were imprisoned. I, Asher, inscribed this...."

Licoricia's son Benedict became the only Jewish guildsman in all of Medieval England. He amassed great wealth and was the only English Jew accorded the same rights as an English subject given to Christians. But even this couldn't save LIcoricia's family from the terrible fate of all English Jews. Another son was executed for the crime of coin-clipping, an accusation that was frequently leveled at English Jews, often baselessly. (Coin clipping was shaving off small amounts of coins and melting down the resulting stolen metal scraps.)

In 1290, all of England's approximately 3,000 Jews were expelled from the country and banned from ever returning. (Jews were only allowed to live in England once more in 1656.) Licoricia's descendents, like most of the English Jews, likely moved to France.

Licoricia new statue in Winchester depicts her standing erect and looking bold, holding the hand of one of her young sons. The base is inscribed in Hebrew and English with the words from Torah: "Love thy neighbor as thyself" (Leviticus 19:18). At long last, Licoricia is remembered once more in her town; her statue is a fitting tribute to a woman who helped support her Jewish community, and who deserves to be remembered today.

Dona Gracia Nasi
1510 - 1569

From the moment of her birth, Gracia Hanasi led a double life: born into a secret Jewish family living in Portugal in 1510, she was bestowed the royal-sounding name of Beatrice de Luna – with Gracia Nasi as her secret Jewish name.

The Nasi family were merchants who likely had fled the Spanish Inquisition in 1492. When Jews were expelled from Portugal in 1495, many declined to move a second time, becoming "Conversos": supposed converts to Christianity in public who maintained Jewish lives in private. The Portuguese authorities were more lenient to these secret Jews than their counterparts in Spain, and Gracia's family were pillars of the secret Jewish community there. In fact, their hidden last name Nasi, meaning "Prince", indicates they were communal leaders. While maintaining an outward appearance of being Christian, the family observed Shabbat, avoided non-kosher foods, and studied Jewish texts in secret.

When she was 18, Gracia married Francisco Mendes, another secret Jew, and together they built up a large trading company. They had one daughter whom they gave two names: Brianda as a non-Jewish name, and Reyna as a secret name. After only eight years of marriage, in 1536, Francisco died. That same year, Portuguese authorities began to crack down on secret Jews, and set up a Holy Office of the Inquisition, modeled after Spain's fearsome religious police. Many of Portugal's secret Jews fled, including Gracia and Reyna.

They settled in Antwerp, which was more tolerant of Jewish practice, and where Gracia had many relatives. Gracia went into business with a brother-in-law, but she longed to move somewhere where she could live completely openly as a Jew. As an upper class businesswoman in Flanders, Gracia knew it would be impossible to run a large business if she openly professed her Jewish faith. Instead, Gracia and her brother-in-law discussed moving to the German lands to the south where communities of Jews lived freely. They set a goal of moving within a year. Sadly, Gracia's brother-in-law died suddenly, making her the sole surviving partner in a large trading company, putting Gracia's plans to move on hold.

She still couldn't live openly as a Jew herself, but Gracia began to use her extensive business contacts to help other Jews escape to cities where they could live Jewish lives. She helped secret Jews escape from Portugal and Spain, and hired guides to help some make the difficult journey over the Alps into Italy or into the Balkans.

In fact, Gracia's extensive business contacts hid a network of escape routes throughout Europe. While she traded spices and gems, her business agents also ferried secret Jews across borders along with this merchandise.

One popular route was for Jews to board Gracia's ships in Spain and Portugal, bound for England. When the ships docked in Southampton or Plymouth, one of Gracia's London agents, a man named Christopher Fernandes, was instructed to board the ships and let the hidden Jews know whether it was safe to stay on board for the next leg of the journey, to the Netherlands. Because Jews were banned from England at the time, the journey was a hazardous one. Another of Gracia's London agents was Antonio de la Ronha, a relative of hers and a learned Jewish scholar. He was tasked with helping Jewish refugees recover property they'd been forced to leave behind.

Once in the Netherlands, many secret Jews found employment in Gracia's warehouses and businesses until they could be dispatched to safety further south to Italy or Turkey. Gracia's agents instructed the fleeing Jews on which roads to travel and in which inns it was safe to stay. They relied on a network of sympathetic allies. In Venice, a non-Jewish printer named Daniel Bomberg, who specialized in printing Hebrew books, received the property of fleeing Jews and returned it to their owners once they'd made it to the relative safety of Italy.

British historian Cecil Roth noted (writing in 1946) that Gracia was the "brains behind the whole of this elaborate organization" and that "There is nothing similar in Jewish history, or perhaps in any history, until our own day and the organization of the 'underground railway' for saving Jews from the hell of Nazi and post-Nazi Europe and securing their entry…to the Land of Israel." (Of course, the American Underground Railroad did help ferry tens of thousands of enslaved Americans to freedom in the North, much as Gracia's extensive network of underground helpers helped to ferry Jews.)

In Antwerp, Gracia's vast wealth attracted unwanted attention from kings and princes. Emperor Charles V wanted Gracia's daughter to marry one of his courtiers so he could seize the family's wealth. To escape this plot, Gracia said she wished to visit a spa in France and fled with her daughter and as much property as they could carry. From France, they traveled on to Italy, settling in Venice where Gracia re-established her trading business.

Even though Jews lived openly in Venice – confined to a dreary island called the Ghetto – Gracia was still not able to reveal her Jewishness publicly: to do so would have meant an end to her business dealings. In fact, it appears Gracia was arrested and held in prison briefly in Venice after she was accused of being a secret Jew. She began a clandestine plan to transfer her wealth to Turkey, with an eye to eventually living there. Turkey at the time was welcoming the Jews who'd been forced out of Europe. Sultan Bajazet II famously declared that he couldn't understand the motives of King Ferdinand of Spain, who'd decreed that all Jews leave Spain in 1492. "How can you call this Ferdinand 'wise' – he who has impoverished his dominions in order to enrich mine?" the Sultan asked as industrious, educated Jews left Europe for Ottoman lands.

Gracia's life in Venice was precarious. In 1550 Venetian authorities started prosecuting secret Jews and Gracia, along with her sister-in-law, daughter and niece, fled to the Italian town of Ferrara. There, for the first time in her life, she publicly declared her Jewishness, using her name Gracia. She changed her last name to her family's previous Hebrew surname of Nasi. When her nephew Joao visited Gracia, he adopted the name Nasi too and changed his first name to Samuel. In Ferrara, Gracia supported local Jewish scholars and paid for the first translation of the Torah into Spanish.

This peace and happiness was short-lived. In 1551, plague broke out in Ferrara. City officials blamed the Jews and forced Jews to leave the town. Gracia decided the time had come. She set sail for Constantinople, in the heart of the Ottoman Empire. There, she set up a fine household, again living openly and proudly as a Jew. She continued to run her trading empire with its secret routes ferrying Jews to freedom, but for the first time Gracia was able to publicly support Jews and Jewish organizations as well.

Each day, 80 poor people entered her grand palace to receive free meals. Gracia paid to redeem Jewish slaves who'd been seized by pirates, a common occurrence at the time. When Turkey experienced a bitterly cold winter in 1567, she paid to help the Ottoman Empire's poor Jews afford heat and clothes. She supported hospitals, charities, schools and synagogues throughout the Ottoman lands.

One of Gracia's favorite projects was a synagogue and yeshiva she established in the heart of Constantinople, known as "the Synagogue of the *Senora*". Previously, local tradition dictated that Constantinople's Jews always prayed in the one synagogue to which their families belonged. Gracia's synagogue was different: it was open to all Jews, welcoming everyone whether they were a member or not.

In 1559, Gracia established a synagogue in Salonika, in Greece, a city in which many secret Jews from Spain were finding refuge. Known as the "Gracia" synagogue, this too was specifically open to all Jews, whether members or not. She also established a *kollel*, or rabbinic academy, in Salonika, where the city's rabbis and scholars could take turns studying Jewish texts full time.

Perhaps Gracia's most ambitious project was supporting the Jewish community in Israel. She petitioned the Sultan for permission to resettle Spanish Jews in Tiberias, an ancient city in the north of Israel, and he agreed. Gracia backed the venture and built a thriving Jewish settlement there, as well as supporting Jews elsewhere in the region. She had a grand house built for herself in Tiberias and petitioned the Sultan for permission to go to the Holy Land.

First, Gracia had a promise to keep. Years before, she'd promised her husband Francisco that she'd do everything in her power to see he was buried in Israel. Now, with great difficulty, she had his body removed from the church graveyard in Lisbon where it was interred and brought to Israel, where he was reburied in Tiberias.

Sadly, Gracia never had the chance to follow him there. She grew sick and withdrew from public life, living in Constantinople in old age in precarious health. She died in about the year 1569, one of the most beloved figures in the entire Jewish world.

Tributes were delivered to Gracia the Nasi throughout Europe and the Middle East. One of the most famous was a poem written by the great Jewish poet Sa'adiah Longo, who had fled the Spanish Inquisition as a child and moved to Salonika with his family. There he witnessed Gracia's generosity and help for her fellow Jews firsthand. In his ode "Dona Gracia of the House of Nasi," he compares Gracia's passing to some of the major calamities in Jewish history. She "straightened the path in the wilderness...the passage to an awesome God," he recalled. That passageway that Gracia Nasi prepared allowed unknown thousands of Jews to escape persecution and death at the hands of the Inquisition and build new lives in safety.

Rivke Tiktiner
Died 1609

Picture of Old Jewish Cemetery, Prague

"She preached day and night to women in every faithful city…" So reads the inscription on an old, crooked tombstone in Prague's old Jewish cemetery, marking the final resting place of Rivke Tiktiner, a teacher, poet, and writer whose words continue to inspire Jews to this day.

Many of the details of Rivke Tiktiner's life have been lost to history. We know she was the daughter of a learned man named Meir, known as *Morenu h'Rav Rabbi* - "Our Teacher and Master, Rabbi" - who ensured that she was highly educated. Rivke was fluent in Hebrew, Yiddish, Aramaic, and other languages, and would go on to write penetrating comments on ideas found in the Torah and Talmud. Her last name, Tiktiner, likely referred to the northeastern Polish town of Tykocin, near Bialystok. It's possible Rivke grew up there, but she lived much of her adult life in Prague, where she was a revered teacher and writer. She was married to a man who was likely not a rabbi. Whether she had children is unknown today.

As her tombstone states, Rivke became a Jewish leader in her own right; her fame was not tethered to an illustrious family or spouse. Contemporary documents refer to her as a *rabbanit*, a female teacher, and a *darshan v'rabbanit*, a preacher and teacher. These honorifics might sound radical today, but from the Middle Ages on, it was common for learned female scholars in Europe to guide and teach their fellow Jewish women. Women called *fizogerin* led prayers in the women's sections of synagogues. After the invention of moveable type printing presses in the 1400s, Jewish books and pamphlets began to be mass-produced; some of these were written by women.

By the time Rivke was preaching and teaching in the late 1500s, it was becoming common to write, print and disseminate Yiddish-language prayers, called *Tehinot*, primarily aimed at women. Instead of the formal Hebrew-language prayers of Jewish liturgy, *Tehinot* were often intimate, designed to be recited before traditionally female activities such as lighting Shabbat candles, sending children off to school, or making the blessing that is recited over challah dough. "As authors, Jewish women held equal status with their male counterparts," notes Yiddish scholar Dr. Devra Kay. *Tehinot* were embraced by Jewish men and women alike, though their informal nature and the fact that Jewish men already were responsible for saying extensive Hebrew prayers three times a day meant that the bulk of *Tehinot* were embraced by women.

Rivke Tiktiner was among the authors to write *Tehinot*, likely in both Hebrew and Yiddish. One of her works survives today, *Shir L'Simchat Torah*, a Song for the Jewish holiday of Simchat Torah, written in Hebrew: it was designed to be said before the holiday even started, when Jewish women went to the synagogue and began to decorate the Torah scrolls for the coming festival. Her prayer seems meant to be sung responsively, or perhaps with women repeating each line after the *fizogerin*. Each line ends with the word *Hallelujah*, or "Praise God".

Here is a sample:

One is our God; You are my Lord. Hallelujah!
Who created my soul and body for me. Hallelujah!
Therefore Your praise will last forever. Hallelujah!
You have always Been and will always Be. Hallelujah!

A prodigious Jewish scholar, Rivke was familiar not only with Hebrew and Yiddish: she also could read Judeo-Arabic, the vernacular language of Spanish Jews. She translated into Yiddish a book from Judeo-Arabic, *Chovot Ha'Levavot*, or "Duties of the Heart," which was written in the 12th Century by Rabbi Bahya ibn Paquda. This work weaves together meditations on Jewish texts with exhortations to recognize God's primacy in our lives and to work to become better people. The book's earnest, encouraging tone seemed to appeal to Rivke and possibly informed her own philosophy and work.

Rivke wrote a book of her own, which is widely considered to be the first printed book authored by a Jewish woman. She titled it *Meineket Rivkah* in a play on her own name, Rivke. (In the Torah, Deborah is described as a righteous, loving woman who served as the wet-nurse - *meineket* - to the Biblical Matriarch Rebecca, Rivke Tiktiner's namesake.)

Meineket Rivkah contains 36 chapters dealing with all aspects of Jewish life, referencing the Torah, Talmud and Jewish commentaries and stories. It is still a stirring call to live a dignified, generous, righteous life today. Rivke opened the volume with a poem, describing the spiritual quest that led her to pen her own book:

....I found a well...and drank from it, but was still thirsty. I said in my heart, then I will go there and bring it to my neighbors, both men and women, enough to drink throughout their entire lives....

In Jewish literature, the Torah is consistently compared to water. Finding the books that were available to her lacking, Rivke was determined to bring the flowing springs of her exalted religious knowledge to her fellow Jews. She wrote her book in Yiddish, the primary language of the Jewish women for whom she toiled.

Her thirty-six chapters describe an exalted life, containing numerous references to the spiritual importance of Jewish women. "It is a sign of blessing to have a daughter as firstborn," Rivke writes, urging her readers that "every woman should make sure that she herself should guide her daughter in good deeds." Distilling the exalted language of the Bible, Rivke concludes "In Yiddish (that is, in the vernacular her readers used every day): this means you should teach your children

Torah." She encourages readers to be generous and quick to help others, and reminds them that anger and hatred have no place in a Jewish home.

Rivke Tiktiner died on the 25th of Nissan (13th of April), 1609, in Prague. Her book *Meineket Rivkah* was published posthumously later that year; another version was issued in 1618. At the conclusion of her book, Rivke notes that "An old woman who is righteous, and does as I have written, will make peace in her tent, and she will also merit having peace in the world to come." Those beautiful words are a fitting tribute to Rivke herself, a giant of a woman about whom we know little today, but whose passion and dedication continue to burn brightly through the beautiful prayers and words she created.

Asnat Barzani
c 1590 - c 1670

Asnat Barzani's grave in Amedi, Iraq

"I never left the entrance to my house or went outside, I was like a princess of Israel... I grew up on the laps of scholars, anchored to my father, of blessed memory.... I was never taught any work but sacred study to uphold, as it is said, 'And you shall recite it day and night' (Joshua 1:8)." - Asnat Barzani

Asnat (sometimes spelled Osnat) Barzani (alternatively sometimes spelled Barazani) did indeed grow up like a princess, a term she often used to reference herself, and did devote her days and nights to sacred study. She was a *bat Melech*, a daughter of a King. (The phrase is used in Judaism to refer to righteous women who are cognizant that they are daughters of the supreme King of the world, and who conduct themselves with dignity and modesty.) From her earliest childhood,

Asnat was recognized as a precious and rare genius by her famous rabbinic family, and educated as such.

Her father was Rabbi Shmuel Adoni Barzani, the chief rabbi of the city of Mosul in the Kurdish region of northern Iraq. At the time, the city was likely home to several thousand Jews and was known as an intensely pious community. Asnat's grandfather had been the revered sage Rabbi Nathanel Adoni Barzani, known as "The Holy." Asnat's father, Rabbi Shmuel, expanded his father's influence, establishing several yeshivas across the region near Mosul. He was widely considered a genius with a talent for teaching Torah.

When it came time to pass on his legacy, it might have seemed to some that Rabbi Shmuel Barzani's influence had come to an end: blessed with no sons, he might have conformed to social expectations and considered himself the last in his family's long rabbinic line. Instead, Rabbi Shmuel Barzani made a remarkable decision, educating Asnat, his only child, as he would have taught a son, molding her into a Jewish scholar who could succeed him in running his yeshivas and providing spiritual guidance to Mosul's Jews. Shockingly, Asnat was soon referred to as "The Tannait," a lofty title that is used for sages in the Mishna and is not applied to other scholars in contemporary times. It was an extraordinary way of referring to any scholar, let alone a woman.

As she described, Asnat rarely left her home, spending her days immersed in Jewish study. She was excused from all household duties and chores. When she was of age, Asnat married a fellow scholar Rabbi Ya'akov Mizrahi, and had an unusual clause in her marriage contract: Asnat was never to be expected to perform any housework so that she could devote herself entirely to learning Torah.

After her father's death, Asnat and her husband Ya'akov ran the Mosul yeshiva together. In a letter written in Hebrew and full of learned references to Jewish texts in the Torah, Bible and Midrash, Asnat described their unusual betrothal and their working partnership in the yeshiva: "(My father) made my husband promise that he would not make me perform work, and (my husband) did as (my father) commanded him. From the beginning, the rabbi (my husband, Ya'akov Mizrahi) was busy with his studies and had no time to teach the pupils, so I taught them in his stead. I was a helpmate for him. (I undertook to garner support for) the sake of my father...and the rabbi...so that their Torah and names should not be brought to naught in these communities (of Kurdistan)." Asnat and Ya'akov had two children together, a daughter and son.

Asnat outlived her husband, and continued to run the Mosul yeshiva alone. Sadly, the school was constantly faced with financial problems, and Asnat spent many hours writing letters to Jewish communities far and wide, asking for funds. "I will cry out for Torah and sigh," she wrote in one typical fundraising letter, using the lyrical Hebrew she was accustomed to; "There is no limit to my desire... The spark of light ignites the cloudy haze... I call to you, my friends, I beseech you... I count on your generous spirit... Raise the rays of light...that Torah should not be extinguished" from Kurdistan because of lack of funds.

In one letter, Asnat wrote of having her own personal possessions taken by debtors, so heavy was the financial burden she carried for the yeshiva. "Nevertheless, I still continue to teach Torah, speaking on the subjects of family purity, tefillah (prayer), Shabbat, and similar topics," she concluded.

The Mosul yeshiva was so renown that in 1630, Rav Pinchas Hariri of Baghdad, some 250 miles south, wrote to Asnat, asking her to send a rabbinic authority to Baghdad to lead the Jewish community there: "My rabbi teacher, we are always willing to serve you with pure faith," Rav Hariri wrote to Asnat. In response, Asnat sent her own son Shmuel, named after her father, to Baghdad, where he became a famed and beloved rabbi. (The Barzani family remained a leading rabbinic family in Baghdad well into the 1700s.)

Asnat became personally revered, both in her lifetime and particularly after her death. She wrote a famous prayer, *Ga'agua L'Zion*, or "Longing for Zion", which allowed many Jews to put their deepest hopes and desires into words of prayer. After her death in about the year 1670, a number of mystic legends sprung up about her. One famous story goes that Asnat magically prevented a synagogue in Mosul from burning in a fire by summoning a flock of angels who put out the flames with their wings. As this and other legends sprung up, her religious writings were treated as holy texts by some Kurdish Jews.

She continues to be known through her writings. Asnat Barzani ensured that Kurdistan's Jews continued to have a top-quality school and a vibrant Jewish life, devoting her entire life to the betterment of her community's Jews. Her tefillot and her example live on, inspiring Kurdish Jews today. Her legacy and remarkable achievements deserve to be better known.

Sarra Copia Sullam
1592-c1651

(Image of the Jewish Ghetto in Venice)

The word "ghetto" originated in Venice. In the Middle Ages, over a dozen bronze foundries were located on a small island in the city. The work required fires and was so dangerous in an urban setting that the metalworks were forced to relocate outside the city. The land where the foundries once stood was damp and undesirable and stood empty for years. In 1516 the Venice city governors voted to relocate all Jews in the city to the cramped island of Ghetto, offering them security, in return for their freedom.

Thousands of Jews eventually moved into the Ghetto. During the day, Jews were allowed to do business throughout Venice, but at sundown they were required to return and were locked in for the night. Metal gates barred passage across the island's only link to the rest of Venice; the Jewish community was forced to pay the very guards who manned the gates and imprisoned them. The only exception to the Jews' nightly curfew were Jewish doctors, who were allowed to leave the Ghetto after dark if they were summoned to treat a gentile patient.

Venice's Jews faced myriad other restrictions, as well. They had to wear yellow hats and other garments, and could practice only a small handful of professions. For many years, it was illegal to study the Talmud in Venice. Yet even these stultifying conditions offered Venetian Jews relative freedom compared to many other locales. Jews moved to Venice from throughout Italy, as well as Spain, Portugal, Germany and elsewhere. The Ghetto hummed with activity and intellectual debate. Five synagogues bustled with prayer and study every day. By 1650, approximately 4,000 Jews lived in the Ghetto, and nearly a third of all the Hebrew language books published in Europe were published in Venice.

Sarra Coppia Sullam was born into this heady environment in the year 1592. Her father, Simone, was a successful Sephardi trader who died when Sarra was fourteen years old. Sarra is buried in Venice's Jewish cemetery next to her father, who educated his daughters and specified in his will that they were free to marry whomever they pleased. In another empowering gesture, Sarra's father named his wife - Sarra's mother - as the executor of his will. He also specified that his family send an annual donation to poor Jews living in the Land of Israel.

Little is known today about Sarra's personal life. She married very young and her husband, Jacob Sullam, was a banker and a prominent leader of the Venetian Jewish community. Sarra gave birth to a daughter who died before her first birthday. After a subsequent miscarriage, Sarra and Jacob were never able to have more children.

It's likely that as wealthy, prominent people, Sarra and Jacob had a relatively spacious room in one of the buildings ringing the two courtyards of the Jewish Ghetto. Yet even for those comfortably off, the Ghetto was terribly overcrowded. Unable to build outside the confines of the Ghetto, Venetian Jews built up, adding story upon story to existing buildings. The Venetian Ghetto contains the world's earliest "skyscrapers": seven and eight story apartment buildings built at a time when such heights were unheard of for residential buildings. With thousands of people confined to such a small area, the buildings were cramped. More than one large family often lived together in a single room.

At night, when the Ghetto gates swung shut and were locked by the island's guards, Sarra and Jacob – like all their friends and relatives – were unable to leave, forced to pace the cramped courtyards with thousands of other Jews if they wished to leave their small, dark living quarters and get some fresh air.

A sense of the rich intellectual world that Sarra inhabited can be gained by taking a look at the work of Rabbi Yehudah Aryeh de Modena (also known as Rabbi Leon Modena) (1571-1648). The Sullams and the Modenas socialized together, and Sarra was a congregant and a disciple of Rabbi Modena. Biographer Rabbi Hersh Goldwurm notes that Rabbi Modena "had an astoundingly versatile mind, and became expert in such diverse subjects as music, mathematics, philosophy, science, etc. He spoke and wrote Italian and Latin fluently, wrote good poetry, and was an expert orator. Above all, he was a master of Jewish learning, and was considered to be one of the foremost (rabbinic leaders) in Italy." Like Rabbi Modena, it seems that Sarra also enjoyed a rich and varied intellectual life, allowing her a way to escape the confines of the Ghetto's walls, if only in her mind.

Outside the Ghetto, Venice teemed with gatherings of intellectuals.

Literary salons were fashionable across Europe during Sarra Copia's life. These were formal gatherings at a specified time each week or month, where people would gather to share poetry, listen to lectures, and debate great themes of the day. The most famous literary salon in Venice took place while wearing masks, affording participants the chance to remain anonymous while they shared controversial opinions. A handful of salons in Venice had been led by Christian women through the decades: Isotta Nogarola (1418-1466), Cassandra Fedele (1465-1558), Vittoria Colonna (1490-1547) and others led successful salons. But doing so could be dangerous for women; historian Lynn Lara Westwater has noted that "while these women earned recognition for their literary skill, male associates often responded to them with slander, sexual interest, or indifference.

In 1618, when she was about 27 years old, Sarra Copia took a shocking step: imitating the Christian women of Venice, she opened her own monthly literary salon inside the Jewish Ghetto. Despite its unique location, Sarra's salon was an instant success, with prominent intellectuals gathering in Sarra's home to hear her speak, to exchange ideas, listen to poetry, and play games. Prof. Howard Adelman of Queens University in Ontario describes the scene: "There was a stream of distinguished visitors – from Treviso, Padua, Vicenza, and beyond (who) congregated because she was a brilliant conversationalist…" Her salon was so impressive that the priest Angelico Aprosio, who was a member of Venice's most prestigious literary salons, called Sarra's gatherings an *accademia*, an academy.

The novelist Nancy Ludmerer vividly imagines what Sarra's salons might have been like: "We read and discuss works-in-progress, philosophy, religion. Sometimes we play music or sing. I decide the order of events - a delicate matter - and when appropriate, express my opinions…Often, I am the only Jew; invariably the only woman. On religious matters, I am outnumbered and outmanned. Nonetheless, I hold my ground." (quoted from *Sarra Copia: A Locked-In Life* by Nancy Ludmerer: 2023).

Yet soon, the Sarra's brilliance attracted unwanted - and dangerous - attention.

Among Sarra's first unwanted suitors was Ansaldo Ceba (1565-1623), a poet who lived in a monastery in the Italian city of Genoa. He and Sarra never met, but they carried out a public literary discourse with one another – until, it seems, Ceba fell in love with Sarra.

Around the time that Sarra opened her salon, she began reading Ceba's poems. One was a long epic called *Queen Esther* about the Biblical Jewish heroine, which Sarra praised highly. She wrote to Ceba, saying she enjoyed his poem so much, she slept with it underneath her pillow. Ceba began to entertain the idea that somehow he and Sarra could be together. Sarra's maiden name was Coppia and she used it in her writing. *Coppia* means couple in Italian, and Ceba wrote her a long letter musing on how appropriate her maiden name was, describing how the two pp's in the middle of her name were like two Christians who were married to one another. Even though he was a monk and Sarra was married (and Jewish), Ceba wrote that he hoped he could convert her and that they could live together happily as a Christian couple like those two p's.

Sarra continued her public correspondence with Ceba – it boosted both of their literary profiles – but she immediately changed the spelling in her maiden name, removing a p and henceforth going by the name Copia.

Sarra soon got into more serious trouble with another Catholic cleric, Baldassare Bonifaccio (1585-1659), the Archdeacon of the town of Treviso, who spent much of his time in Venice.. Bonifaccio attended Sarra's salon and eventually put her life in peril.

At one of Sarra's salons, participants discussed the immortality of the soul. Afterwards, Bonifaccio wrote a long *Discorso* (discourse) on the immortality of souls and accused Sarra of not believing in this core Christian and Jewish tenet. He suggested that she convert to Christianity and thus resolve her supposed blasphemy. This was a grave charge in 17th century Italy, and Sarra was terrified that Bonifaccio's baseless accusation could harm the entire Jewish community. Bonifaccio's slander could give the Roman Inquisition an excuse to try Sarra and perhaps even other Jews in Venice. None of the people who frequented Sarra's salon came to her defense.

Sarra took to her room and spent two days penning a response. The result was magnificent: her *Manifesto* drew on Jewish and secular writings to marshal arguments for belief in the immortality of the soul. Sarra railed against Bonifaccio's betrayal in accusing her of heresy, and dissected his arguments one by one. Sarra poured her entire being into this *Manifesto*; she even included four of her sonnets as she built her case, defending her Jewish beliefs, and expressing her hurt that Bonifaccio had endangered her and the entire Jewish community. The work was designed to protect the entire Venetian Jewish community from the baseless accusation that Sarra - and by extension, her family, friends, and religious community - were apostates.

The *Manifesto* was an instant success. (It's full name in English was *The Manifesto of Sarra Copia Sulam, a Jewish Woman, In Which She Refutes and Disavows the Opinion Denying Immortality of the Soul, Falsely Attributed to Her by Mr. Baldassare Bonifacio.*) Readers throughout Venice and beyond bought all the copies that Sarra printed and read and debated her points in many other literary salons. Her *Manifesto* was re-issued several times, as printers tried to keep up with demand for Sarra's work.

Bonifaccio accused Sarra of not being the *Manifesto's* author, claiming that Rabbi Modena must have written it. Yet Bonifaccio never responded to Sarra's criticisms, merely maintaining in his public correspondence that she ought to convert to Christianity.

Sarra's salon continued for only a few years, until 1624. During that time, she was able to converse with educated, fascinating people from throughout Venice who all made the trek to the Jewish Ghetto. Sarra's many poems continued to be well received and often read. Yet as a public figure, Sarra was slandered by the Christian men who attended her salon. Her rivals accused her of sexual impropriety and plagiarism, and bribed her servants to spy on her and bring salacious reports of supposed immorality in her household. Sarra spent years watching as her name was dragged through the mud by writers who concocted outrageous, grotesque, and damaging stories about her supposedly outlandish love life.

It's not known if Sarra eventually regretted opening her home to others who would later turn on her so viciously. She lived to about 49 and never stopped writing. She and Jacob never left Venice's Jewish Ghetto. By the end of Sarra's life, her literary salon, and her public correspondence with some of the greatest thinkers of the day, were nothing but long-distant memories.

Sarra died as she was born: hemmed in by the Ghetto's gates, allowed to live not with the Gentiles she debated and corresponded with, but with the Jewish community she tried so strenuously to protect when her fame put her coreligionists in danger. That, and Sarra's beautiful literary works, some of which survive today, are her legacy to us.

Gluckel of Hameln
1646 - 1724

Gluckel was one of countless Jewish women who worked as a merchant in Germanic lands: one of many who lived a pious life, was involved in her Jewish community, and had business dealings across a great area. Unlike most of these unknown women whose names and legacies have been lost to history, Gluckel of Hameln penned a stirring memoir that has survived through the ages. Its pages bring Gluckel to life in all her vivacity, and offer us a glimpse into the world she inhabited.

Born in 1646 in Hamburg, Gluckel was two when the long, bloody Thirty Years War ended. Ravaged by the war, which inflamed religious passions as Protestants and Catholics battled one another, German rulers were often in no mood to treat their Jewish subjects well. In Hamburg, Lutheran preachers called synagogues "churches of Satan" and fomented anti-Jewish hatred.

When Gluckel was three years old, Hamburg expelled its Jews. Most Jewish families moved to the nearby town of Altona, which was controlled by Denmark's King Frederick III, and was more hospitable to Jews. Gluckel provides a sense of the hardship involved:

After we newcomers had remained there for some time, we finally succeeded with great difficulty in persuading the authorities of Hamburg to grant passes to Altona

Jews, so we might enter and do business in that city. Such a pass was valid for four weeks; it was issued by the burgermeister and cost one ducat; when it expired another had to be procured in its stead…

She records how some poor Jews, in desperate need to return to their places of business, slipped into Hamburg without the requisite pass. If they were caught, they were thrown into prison, and the entire local Jewish community had to pay a fine to get them out.

In the early dawn, as soon as our folds were out of synagogue, they went down to Hamburg, and towards evening, when the gates were closed, back they came to Altona. Coming home, our poor folks often took their life in their hands because of the hatred for the Jews rife among the dockhands, soldiers and others of the meaner classes. The good wife, sitting home, often thanked God when her husband turned up safe and sound.

Gluckel describes her family as intensely pious and bastions of Hamburg's Jewish community. "My father dealt in precious stones and other wares like a Jew who knows how to turn everything to account," she describes. When Jews were finally allowed to return to live in Hamburg, he was the first one to settle there. Gluckel doesn't describe her education, but it clearly was extensive: an intensely religious woman, she fills her memoirs with quotes and references to the Jewish Bible and to Midrash (Jewish aggadic tales). Her memoirs are written in Yiddish, and it seems that she lived her long life, flourishing both in business and social spheres, entirely in that language.

She describes the horrific problems that beset Jews at the time in matter of fact terms, for hardship and uncertainty marked Gluckel's whole life. She describes how her grandfather, Nathan Melrich, arrived in Hamburg because he was driven out of the town of Detmold. He and some of his children died in a plague, and Gluckel's grandmother and two of her children wandered the countryside, receiving no aid from any quarter.

In 1648, the Cossack leader Bogdan Chmielnicki raised an army in Ukraine to fight against their Polish overlords. Rampaging across Ukraine, all the way to the city of Lviv, the Chmielnicki Uprising saw hordes of Cossack soldiers unleash terrible barbarity on everyone in their way. They particularly hated Jews, and destroyed 300 Jewish communities between 1648 and 1649, murdering 100,000 Jews.

Some of the desperate Jewish refugees from these massacres made it to Hamburg, and Gluckel's family took them in. "Many of them, stricken with contagious diseases, found their way to Hamburg," Gluckel records; "Having as yet neither hospital nor other accommodations, we needs must bring the sick among them into our homes. At least ten of them, whom my father took under his charge, lay in the upper floor of our house. Some recovered; others died."

Gluckel's elderly grandmother insisted on climbing the stairs to minister to the refugees many times each day. Gluckel and her sister Elkele became sick, and their grandmother also took ill and died.

Betrothed at age 12, Gluckel married Chayim Hameln when she was 14 years old. She describes her loneliness and sense of dislocation following the marriage:

Immediately afterwards my parents returned home and left me - I was a child of scarcely fourteen - alone with strangers in a strange world. That it did not go hard with me I owed to my new parents who made my life a joy. Both dear and godly souls, they cared after me better than I deserved. What a man he was, my father-in-law, like one of God's angels!

Hameln, everyone knows what it is compared to Hamburg; taken by itself, it is a dull shabby hole. And there I was - a carefree child whisked in the flush of youth from parents, friends and everyone I knew, from a city like Hamburg plopped into a back-country town where lived only two Jews"

Gluckel and Chaim went into the gemstone trade, like so many Jewish families in the region, and soon moved to Hamburg where there were more business opportunities. They had 14 children (two of whom died in infancy), and Gluckels' memoirs are filled with details about her household arrangement, their business partnerships, and local gossip from the Jewish community. Together, Gluckel and

Chaim married off four of their children; Gluckel took great pride in finding matches among some of the most prominent Jewish families in Europe for them.

During the winter of 1689, Chaim was walking through town when he slipped and fell. He returned home in great agony, and tried to hide his injuries but to no avail. As the days passed, Chaim became sicker and sicker. The doctors at the time relied on "cures" like bloodletting, and soon it was clear that Chaim wasn't long for this world. Gluckel called for one of Chaim's good friends to visit the dying man; his friend asked Chaim if he had any last wishes to instruct his family and friends. "None. My wife knows everything. She shall do as she has always done," Chaim said. He then asked for a Jewish book, and spent half an hour studying Torah. That night, Chaim died. Gluckel had lost her "dear friend" and was distraught.

What shall I write, dear children, of all our bitter grief? I had always stood so high in his eyes, and now I was abandoned with eight of my twelve forlorn children - and one of them, my daughter Esther, betrothed! May God have mercy on us and be the Father of my children, for He is the Father of the fatherless! I truly believe I shall never cease from mourning for my dear friend."

Gluckel took over the family business trading gold and seed pearls, and began writing her memoirs. "In my great grief and for my heart's ease I begin this book the year of Creation 5451 (1690-91) - God soon rejoice us and send us His redeemer!" she begins.

Gluckel lived through some of the most consequential events in Jewish history. One was the euphoria that swept European Jewry for Shabbatai Zvi, a fraud from Smyrna in Turkey, who convinced Jews throughout the Middle East and Europe that he was the Messiah. Jews in the Land of Israel, Egypt, Syria, Turkey, Greece and Italy began selling all their possessions in preparation for the Messianic Age. Soon, word that the Messiah had arrived spread to Europe. Gluckel's father in law was a believer.

She describes how news came from Smyrna in Turkey about Shabbatai Zvi's arrival. Hamburg was home to a Sephardic Jewish community, and they embraced Shabbatai Zvi first.

The Sephardic youth came dressed in their best finery and decked in broad green silk ribbons, the gear of Shabbatai Zvi. "With timbrels and with dances" (a reference to celebrations in Exodus 15:20) *they one and all trooped to the synagogue, and they read the letters forth with joy like the "joy of the Feast of Water-Drawings"* (a reference to ancient celebrations of Sukkot).

Many sold their houses and lands and all their possessions, for any day they hoped to be redeemed. My good father-in-law left his home in Hameln, abandoned his house and lands and all his goodly furniture, and moved to Hildesheim. He sent on to us in Hamburg two enormous casks packed with linens and with peas, beans, dried meats, shredded prunes and like stuff, every manner of food that would keep. For the old man expected to sail any moment from Hamburg to the Holy Land.

After a year, it was obvious that Shabbatai Zvi was not the Messiah, and Gluckel opened the casks. (Gluckel, memorably, describes the Jewish people anticipating the "birth pangs of the Messiah" and instead bringing forth a fart.) In 1666, Shabbatai Zvi converted to Islam. The entire experience shook Gluckel, and she urged her children to remain steadfastly pious: 'I am certain God would have mercy on us; if only we kept the commandment "Thou shalt love thy neighbor as thyself! But God forgive us for the way we keep it - no good can come from jealousy and footless hate that rule our lives..."

For years, Gluckel's fortunes flourished. "My business prospered, I procured me wares from Holland, I bought nicely in Hamburg as well, and disposed of the goods in a stores of my own. I never spared myself, summer and winter I was out on my travels, and I ran about the city the livelong day," she describes. She traveled widely, for business and pleasure, visiting Amsterdam, Copenhagen, Hanover, and Berlin. Gluckel attended weddings, met with relatives, negotiated marriages for her children, and expanded her trading network.

In 1770, Gluckel married Hertz Levy, the leader of the Jewish community in Metz. A wealthy banker, he soon suffered a series of misfortunes, went bankrupt, and died in 1711, a broken man. All of Gluckel's money had been tied up in her husband's business, and she was left penniless. "I write this, therefore, with trembling hands and hot bitter tears," Gluckel records in her memoirs as she describes this terrible period in her life. Gluckel had hoped to spend her final years in the land of Israel, but it was not to be. Instead, she moved in with her daughter and son in law in Metz.

Ever the pious optimist, Gluckel found much to enjoy in her new, reduced circumstances. She praises Metz for its highly religious community and friendliness. Her book brims with religious advice to her beloved children. "This, dear children, will be no book of morals," she announces, but her memoirs are replete with religious stories, observations and advice which grew out of the rich Jewish world Gluckel inhabited.

Gluckel's original manuscript was lost, but her son Moshe and her grandson Chaim each made a copy. These family treasures were translated into German for Gluckel's family by her descendant, the Austrian Jewish feminist Bertha Pappenheim in 1896. (Bertha also posed as Gluckel for a painting of her by artist Leopold Pilichowski, pictured at the start of this chapter.) The only current English translation of Gluckel's memoirs, by Marvin Lowenthal, used Bertha's text, but cut much of Gluckel's religious comments, dismissing her Jewish insights as "theologizing." Despite these omissions, Gluckel's life and engaging personality continue to leap off the page, giving us insight into a remarkable Jewish woman and her world.

Temerl Bergson
died 1830

From her earliest years, Temerl Bergson was blessed with wealth, brilliance, an excellent education, and lived in the loving embrace of some of Poland's most dynamic Jewish communities. Her father was called Avraham of Opoczno, a town that at the time was home to a thriving Jewish community; fully a majority of the several thousand people who lived in the town were Jews.

Termerl married young, to a merchant from Warsaw named Jacob. They had a baby boy named Hirsch, but tragically Jacob passed away soon after Hirsch's birth. In 1787, Temerl married again, this time joining one of Polish Jewry's most respected and renowned families.

Her new groom was Berek Bergson, a twenty three year old devout Jew from Praga, a suburb of Warsaw. Berek's father, Shmuel Zbitkower, had earned a fortune as a merchant and was beloved far and wide as a savior of Polish Jewry. (The family, confusingly, adopted different surnames through the years and under different regimes: they were variously known as Zbitkower, Sonenberg, and - after Berek became an influential figure in his own right - as Berkson and Bergson.) Fully a century after Shmuel lived, the Polish-Jewish writer, Zionist and politician Nahum Sokolow reminisced about the stories he'd grown up hearing about Shmuel Zbitkower, Berek and Temerl as a child in Poland.

For instance, Sokolow recalled hearing about the family's actions during the 1794 Battle of Praga, during which Russian troops attacked Warsaw, training their fury on the suburb of Praga, unleashing "a hurricane of brutality...Jewish blood flowed like water," Sokolow described. Russian troops refused to allow the Jews they'd killed to be buried; many Jews who tried to bury their dead were attacked. To prevent some of the worst of the violence, Shmuel "sacrificed his gold and saved a good many Jewish lives," Sokolow recorded hearing. The stories of his noble acts were passed down through the generations.

When Termerl and Berek married, the wedding was held outdoors in bitterly cold February with a distinguished guest list: even King Stanislaw August attended. Temerl's and Berek's marriage seems to have been a joyously happy one, and they would go on to have five children together.

Firmly ensconced in the Bergson family, Temerl showed a natural brilliance for business and expanded the family's holdings and wealth to a breathtaking level, eventually becoming one of the richest people in all of Poland. Termerl also pushed the boundaries of her new clan's religious ideals and philanthropy, becoming a major force in the development and flowering of Chassidic Jewry.

Berek clearly realized what a treasure he'd found in Temerl. "I have long known her to be a clever and just wife, always my bulwark, guarding my person and property. She acted with all her strength for my own good and grace, so much that I cannot express the wisdom with which she built my House, and extended her open hand to the poor and downtrodden. She always delighted in leading my children on a good and just path of God and Man. Praise God that it was the Lord's pleasure that fortune was achieved by her hand, in everything toward which she turned it," he later wrote.

Temerl helped Berek run (and expand) a salt company. She founded a bank that would soon grow into one of Poland's leading financial institutions. In 1810, a now rich Temerl bought a house at 1076 Krolewska Street, one of Warsaw's major boulevards and a thoroughfare in which it was ordinarily forbidden for Jews to dwell: Termerl received special permission to live there, and her husband Berek gained official leave to retain his distinctive Jewish dress, beard and sidelocks, a form of dress that was otherwise prohibited in wealthy sections of Warsaw.

Historian Avraham Rubinstein described Temerl as having "brought Hasidism to her husband's house." Berel was always a devout Jew, but Temerl was drawn to the new Chassidic movement that was sweeping across Poland, with its emphasis on joy, intense religious devotion and personal relationships with charismatic rabbis and tightly-knit Jewish communities. In 1807, she and Berek helped found a Chassidic synagogue and Beit Midrash (Jewish study hall).

After Berek's death in 1822, Temerl ran the family's business empire and expanded it a great deal. In 1827 she petitioned the crown for permission to buy a noble estate, and became only the third Jew in Poland given the right to own landed property. Yet her business acumen hid a much deeper desire: Temerl used her extensive business holdings to support some of the most influential Chassidic rebbeim of her day: some of the Chassidic leaders whose names are today household words in many Jewish homes owe their livelihood to Temerl Bergson.

When the great Chassidic leader Rabbi Simcha Bunim of Peshischa ("Reb Bunim") was a young, brilliant and penniless scholar, Temerl offered him a job as her agent at the Leipzig trade fairs. Reb Bunim worked for Temerl for many years: the "gates of fortune have opened for me" he is said to have exclaimed. Temerl hired Reb Bunim's disciple Reb Israel Yitzhak Kalish of Warka to manage some of her properties.

At her noble estate, Temerl replaced the clerks with Chassidim, giving them a dignified means of supporting themselves and their communities. Historian Glenn Dynner quotes one observer who noted: "They only dedicated a few hours to clerical duties and managing the rich holdings. Temerl did not even demand this. They dedicated the remaining hours of the day and night to Torah and service. From her profits, the wealthy woman (Temerl) established a house of study, whose doors were open day and night."

Temerl wholeheartedly believed that she had become wealthy only in the merit of the good deeds she did for the Jewish community and to help her continue to support poor Jews. In ways large and small, from employing leading Jewish sages to helping arrange the weddings of local Jewish girls, Temerl's life was one of tireless giving. In some quarters, she was given the honorific "Reb." (Usually used to refer to men, this wasn't a feminist gesture, but a sign of the deep appreciation in which Polish Jews held their patroness. When the anti-Chassidic writer Joseph Perl wrote a satire of Chassidic life in which he made fun of Temerl's honorific "Reb," Temerl offered 3 zlotys for every copy she could buy to keep them out of readers' hands.)

Of her six children, only one son, Michal, left the religious life his mother so prized, becoming a musician and popularizing the music of Frederic Chopin in Europe. Her other children remained in the Chassidic fold; Temerl's son Jacob eventually took over most of her business empire. One document has endured, shedding light on the rich material and Jewish life that Temerl and Berek created. In 1806, Temerl and Berek's daughter married in the Polish town of Warka; the city hall still retains an official description of the event:

"The wedding was attended by the Maggid of Kozienice, Reb Israel Hapstein. The Maggid spent two Sabbaths in Warka, the Sabbaths of the weekly Torah readings *Yitro* and *Mishpatim*. On the first Sabbath, he was joined by one hundred guests and followers. Great feasts were held daily, at which Austrian whiskey was served. The Maggid preached words of Torah at these meals, the likes of which had never been heard. During his visit he gave countless sermons (and) urged...that a synagogue be built in town." (Four years later, the Maggid returned to Warka and laid the cornerstone of a new shul.)

Temerl's legacy was remembered for generations in Poland, up to the period before the Holocaust. "The loveliness of a flower, the modesty of a dove, a soul with wings of gold, and fruitful as an olive tree," Nahum Sokolow recalled the descriptions of Temerl he grew up hearing in his youth.

Temerl Bergson's grave still stands, in the Jewish cemetery on Okopowa Street in Warsaw, and recalls her greatness still:

In this Land, a life that was mighty among princes
To her nation she was a protector against oppression - a helper in distress
To the poor she was a mother
She was a virtuous woman, powerful and famous.

Rebecca Gratz
1781 - 1869

Rebecca Gratz's long life embodied contradiction. Born during the American
Revolutionary War, she lived long enough to witness - and be outraged by - the
Civil War which tore both her nation and her family apart. Habituating the upper
echelons of Philadelphia society, Rebecca also was an outsider: a committed Jew
who bore anti-Semitic slights her entire life. Seeking to instruct American Jewish
children, she invented Jewish Sunday school, modeling it on the Protestant Sunday
schools which were becoming popular at the time. Generations of Jewish children
have been educated according to Rebecca's vision.

Her family seems to have conveyed a strong sense of Jewish practice, but without
much of the joy that many people find in Jewish life. Rebecca's father Michael
was born in Silesia and lived in Amsterdam, London and the West Indies before
settling in Philadelphia, along with his brother, in the 1760s. Michael Gratz
married an American-born Jewish woman, Miriam Simon, from Lancaster,
Pennsylvania, and kept a kosher home; Michael declined to do business on
Shabbat. Yet this piety wasn't passed along to the next generation; of the Gratzs'
twelve children, only three married fellow Jews, building new Jewish households
for themselves.

From an early age, Rebecca was drawn to religion. On a river cruise in upstate
New York in 1805, Rebecca wrote to her mother that she had kosher meat

delivered to the ship, that she prayed every morning, and that she fasted for part of the day on the Jewish fast day of *Tisha B'Av*. Her brothers seem to have been less scrupulous in their observances: "Do not get too fond of oysters" she wrote to one on a similar trip when they enjoyed non-kosher delicacies away from home.

The Gratz men were traders and for much of Rebecca's life, her family was wealthy, occupying a grand house in Philadelphia. As a young woman, Rebecca became friends with a celebrated group of writers who contributed to a Philadelphia literary magazine called *Port Folio*, established in 1801: Washington Irving and the grandsons of Alexander Hamilton counted as her close friends. Rebecca confided in friends that she, too, was a writer, penning poetry, but that she gave it up, using her literary talents on letters instead. Throughout her life, Rebecca corresponded with a huge circle of people in America and Britain, and took it upon herself to keep in touch with everyone in her very large extended family, relaying family news.

Though she was part of the avant garde social circle surrounding the *Port Folio*, Rebecca could never escape the sense that as a Jew she was a perennial outsider. In the magazine's very first edition, John Quincy Adams wrote about a tour through Silesia, where Rebecca's father was born: it described Berlin as "an old town…about twelve thousand inhabitants, of which a quarter are…FILTH…Jews." Elsewhere, the magazine had a strongly pro-Christian bent, further reminding Rebecca of her outsider status.

Rebecca had nowhere to turn. She confided her hurt in friends, almost all of whom were Christian, some of whom occasionally tried to convert her. One of her closest friends was Marie Gist Gratz, her brother Ben's non-Jewish wife, in whom Rebecca confided her many disappointments. "Henceforth we will not remember that there is a difference of opinion (in terms of marriage between Christians and Jews) and I trust we will be sincere friends," Rebecca once wrote to her, seemingly reflecting an argument that both women tried imperfectly to mend.

Rebecca never married; her biggest romance was with a Protestant lawyer whom she refused to wed because of the differences in their faiths. It was widely rumored at the time that Rebecca - wealthy, bright, vivacious, beautiful, and stubbornly insistent on not marrying her non-Jewish suitor - was the inspiration for Sir Walter Scott's Jewish heroine Rebecca in his popular 1819 novel *Ivanhoe*. Rebecca Gratz never confirmed nor denied that she inspired this strong Jewish character, though she encouraged the speculation.

Beneath her high-society exterior, Rebecca was a radical reformer, whose radicalism, like her spiritualism, became more pronounced as she aged. When she was nineteen years old, her father suffered a stroke and Rebecca was appointed his nurse and her mother's helper, performing much of the family's household chores. The following year, along with her mother and sister Rachel, Rebecca became a founding member of the Female Association for the Relief of Women and Children of Reduced Circumstances in Philadelphia. This small charity was groundbreaking: of the 23 founding members, eight were Jews; it was the first charity in Philadelphia which was not religiously-based. The charity insisted in its charter that only unmarried women serve as treasurer, so that no husband could ever claim ownership of the charity's funds. Rebecca served as secretary. It was a role she would reprise again and again in the many charitable boards on which she sat. As secretary, Rebecca was able to set agendas and record minutes, and found a powerful way to sway organizations' agendas to her will.

In the mid-1800s, evangelical Christian groups made huge efforts to Christianize American society: by 1860, there were twice as many Christian churches in the United States, per capita, as there had been in 1780. This rise in Christian religious fervor mirrored Rebecca's own growing interest in religion and spirituality. As her commitment to Jewish study intensified, so did Rebecca's desire to save her co-religionists from attempts to convert them to Christianity.

One pressing need was to create Jewish social service organizations. Gratz helped found the Philadelphia Orphan Asylum in 1815. Though she remained committed to this orphanage, and served as its secretary for the next 40 years, Rebecca realized that it couldn't serve the needs of Jewish orphans: orphans were required to say Christian prayers daily and listen to passages from the Christian Bible. Even meetings of the orphanage's board opened with Christian prayers. Rebecca praised these Protestant opening prayers in letters to her friends, but sought to create new services to help Philadelphia's Jewish community.

In 1819, Rebecca became one of the founding members of the Female Hebrew Benevolent Society, a project spearheaded by members of the Orthodox Philadelphia synagogue Rebecca attended, Mikveh Israel. The society provided food, clothes, and wood and coal to poor Jewish families in Philadelphia. They also arranged for doctors and nurses' visits and aided poor Jews in finding work.

Many years later, in 1855, Rebecca campaigned for help founding a Jewish orphanage in Philadelphia. She wrote an open letter in the Jewish newspaper the *Occident* declaring that readers would one day find themselves "at the judgment seat of…God," being judged by how they treat the poor and that "good wishes alone will not avail…helpless children". Signing her letter "a Daughter of Israel," Rebecca pointed out that readers couldn't be sure that they, or their children or grandchildren, might not one day find themselves destitute and in need of aid. Her appeal was successful, and later that year, the Jewish Foster Home and Orphan Asylum was established, with Rebecca on the board. The orphanage and foster home was national in scale, and prioritized placements for Jewish orphans who were being raised in Christian homes.

Though she never married, when Rebecca's sister Rachel passed away in 1823, Rebecca took in Rachel's six children and raised them as her own, heading a large household single-handedly. Rebecca sometimes spoke about wanting to write children's books, and she was close friends with two Philadelphia Jewish women who were devoted teachers: Simha Peixotto and her sister Rachel Reixotto, who ran a ladies academy in Philadelphia. With so many American Jewish children growing up ignorant of their religion - and with the example of the early Christian Sunday School movement to draw on - Rebecca began persuading friends and backers to help her start a weekly Jewish school.

Hers wasn't the first Jewish school in Philadelphia. The Orthodox synagogue Rodeph Shalom had run a Jewish school since 1822. For Rebecca, this wasn't enough. Historian Diane Ashton noted that Rebecca "believed that financial independence alone would not be enough to enable immigrants to live socially respected lives in the United States. Nor would the ability to recite traditional prayers in Hebrew enable a Jewish child to withstand evangelical arguments."

Giving American Jewish children tools to counter Christian evangelists was crucial at the time.

The Hebrew Sunday School opened on March 4, 1838, Rebecca's 57th birthday, with 50 students. Six teachers, including the Peixotto sisters and Rebecca, who also served as superintendent, taught the children. After reciting a prayer that Rebecca composed and listening to her give a sermon, students broke into smaller classes and studied the weekly Torah portion. Rebecca graded students' weekly assignments: penmanship counted as much as the contents of the essays. School was limited to two hours each Sunday morning. By 1841, the school had over a hundred students, which represented between 80% and 90% of all English-speaking Jewish children in Philadelphia at the time. The school was open to all, with no fee.

Rebecca insisted that teachers conduct themselves with utmost propriety, and she encouraged students to honor Shabbat by not attending public school classes on Saturdays. She insisted students learn the *Shema* prayer and read the books of the Hebrew Bible. Perhaps reflecting the highly female nature of the school's teaching staff and leadership, the Biblical books of Esther and Ruth were given prominence in the curriculum. Rebecca also relied heavily on the teaching materials written by another remarkable Jewish woman, Grace Aguillar in England, who was a devout Jew who penned a wide variety of novels, poetry and Jewish religious works.

In 1854, the Hebrew Sunday School moved into the newly opened Touro Hall, endowed by New Orleans Jewish philanthropist Judah Touro, who would go on to develop a Jewish school which taught both Jewish and secular subjects. (When Rebecca's brother Hyman died in 1857, he bequeathed a fund for the establishment of a Jewish teacher's college, Gratz College, which continues to educate a new generation of Jewish leaders and others today.)

Rebecca remained the Hebrew Sunday School's superintendent until 1864, the year before her death, when she stepped down due to ill health. Rebecca called her work with the Hebrew Sunday School the "crowning happiness of my days." Her model of weekly Jewish Sunday school continues to educate Jewish children around the world.

Lady Judith Montefiore
1784 - 1862

It was, in the words of Charles Dickens, "the best of times and the worst of times." While revolution and political strife roiled Continental Europe, Britain in the 1780s and beyond was home to progressive social change, and to a growing community of educated, cultured Jews who flocked to England.

They called themselves the "Cousinhood" – brilliant Jewish families who built empires of business and service, married into each other's dynasties and created a new, vibrant Jewish community. One of the most prominent of these immigrant Jews was the Dutch-born Levi A. Barnet Cohen who moved to London in the 1770's and eventually became one of a dozen Jews newly elected to Parliament, without compromising his Orthodox Jewish faith. He married a brilliant Jewish woman named Lydia and together they raised an observant Jewish family. Their daughter, Lady Judith Montefiore, was born in 1784.

One of seven children, Judith distinguished herself from a young age as a precocious genius and a committed Jew. She learned French, German, Italian, Arabic, and Hebrew, gained mastery in art, music, literature, and regularly studied the weekly Torah portion. From childhood, she learned to occupy two realms: that of the highest levels of English upper-class society, and also that of her deeply held Orthodox Jewish religion.

One of Judith's strongest childhood memories was of a Tisha B'Av, the Jewish day of mourning for the destruction of the ancient Jewish Temple in Jerusalem when

84

it's customary to fast and to sit on low chairs or the floor. She and her sisters were sitting on the ground in her family's grand London house when a servant ushered in a group of visiting gentlemen, including Admiral Sir Sidney Smith, who were looking for her father. The men were startled to find Judith and her sisters sitting on the floor in defiance of social norms and protocols.

"I quietly kept my seat," Judith later recalled, "and when Sir Sidney asked the reason of our being seated so low, I replied, 'This is the anniversary of the destruction of Jerusalem, which is kept by conforming Jews as a day of mourning and humiliation…. The valor exhibited by our ancestors on this sad occasion is no doubt well known to you, Sir Sidney…and I feel sure that you will understand our grief that it was unavailing to save the Holy City and the Temple'."

If Admiral Smith was surprised to be given a lesson in history and the Jewish religion by a child, he didn't show it. Instead he replied that he understood perfectly. Judith later recalled that he "observed that…the memory of the struggles of the Jews in Palestine to remain the rightful masters of the land which God had apportioned to them as an inheritance, would ever remain, not only in the heart of every brave man in the British realm, but also in that of every right-thinking man in all other parts of the world as a glorious monument of their dauntless valor and fervent devotion to a good and holy cause."

Educated and passionate, Judith Cohen waited until relatively late in life to marry: she was 28 when she met Moses Montefiorie, the Italian-born son of a prominent Jewish family which now called England home. Moses was a force of nature: he'd already built, lost and then re-built a fortune as an international merchant. Most of all, he was religiously observant. While many upper-class British Jews were abandoning the trappings of their religion, he and Judith hoped to build a strong, religiously observant Jewish family together.

Judith was Ashkenazi and Moses was Sephardi; though many British Jews of the time did not want to marry outside of their own narrow Jewish tradition, Judith and Moses envisioned a new sort of Jewish life where all Jews were united. Soon after their marriage, they began working to make that vision a reality, supporting Jewish communities in Britain and around the world, and most of all working to rebuild Jewish life in the Land of Israel Judith threw herself into building the Jewish

Ladies' Loan and Visiting Society, a Jewish orphanage in London, and educational programs for girls at Jews' Hospital.

Moses rose in British society. He was knighted in 1837 (Judith gained the honorific Lady then); that year he was also elected the Sheriff of London – only the second Jew ever elected to that post. Yet despite the Montefiore's high social position, they were dogged for years by anti-Semitism and snide anti-Jewish remarks.

An observer recorded the abuse the Montefiores received first-hand. "On Sunday, the Montefiores went to the banquet at the Governor General's," wrote Pauline Wengeroff, a Russian Jewish woman visiting Britain, who was present at the dinner. She had seen the Montefiores the day before, Shabbat, in synagogue, and noted that while the couple wore simple, modest clothing while in synagogue, at this dinner they were resplendent. "Sir Montefiore sat proudly erect in his red Sheriff's uniform with gold stripes...and next to him, Lady Judith in the most magnificent dress of an English lady-in-waiting." A Polish count at the dinner loudly complained to other guests about the supposed cost of Judith's earrings, repeating the old slander that Jews have too much wealth. "Another could not suppress a snide remark, asking why people were making so much fuss about a Jewess."

At another dinner party the Montefiores were seated next to a rabid anti-Semite who told the Montefiores that he had recently returned from Japan where, he said, "they have neither pigs nor Jews." Without missing a beat, Moses is said to have replied that in that case they should both travel there immediately, so that the Japanese could have "a sample of each".

In 1840 anti-Semitism in Britain rose to a fever pitch. That year, an Italian priest and his Muslim servant were murdered in the city of Damascus, then part of the Ottoman Empire. Almost immediately, local authorities accused Damascus' Jews of the double murder. Echoing Medieval blood libels, they accused Jews of killing the pair in order to use their blood to bake Passover matzah. Several Jews were arrested and 63 Jewish children were seized by the Damascus police in order to pressure their parents to confess to the killings.

Despite the patent absurdity of the Damascus Blood Libel, as the affair became known, many anti-Semites in the West seized on it as proof that Jews were somehow evil and not to be trusted. An editorial in the *London Times* in June 1840 declared that the accusation against Damascus' Jews was "one of the most important cases ever submitted to the notice of the civilized world… Admitting for the moment (that the case was justified)...then the Jewish religion must at once disappear from the face of the earth…"

Faced with this crisis, the Montefiores organized a committee of influential Jews and traveled to Damascus to intervene in the charges, persuading local authorities to drop charges against the Jews and to release the Jewish children. They also undertook many other trips to help Jews, including visiting Czar Nicholas I in 1846 to ask him to rescind his decree that prohibited Jews from living in regions of Western Russia, along the area bordering modern day Poland.

Sadly, Judith suffered from ill health; she and Moses were never able to have children. Despite her frequent bouts of sickness, Judith insisted on carrying out a heavy schedule of charitable work and travel. Most important to her and Moses were the five trips they undertook together to visit the Land of Israel, where they agitated for greater rights from the Turkish overlords, and donated funds to the Jewish towns and farms that were beginning to flourish throughout modern day Israel. Women especially came to visit Judith when she was in the Land of Israel, asking for alms, which she willingly gave.

On her first visit to Israel, in 1836, Judith prayed at the Tomb of the Biblical Matriarch Rachel, just outside of Jerusalem. She "was deeply impressed with a feeling of awe and respect, standing as I did, in the sepulcher of a mother of Israel," she wrote in her diary. She also remarked that she was only one of six European women to have visited the holy site in the previous century. When she visited the Western Wall in Jerusalem, she recorded her feeling "a sentiment of veneration and interest amounting to awe."

The Montefiores visited Israel again two years later, where they helped rebuild a synagogue in Safed which had been destroyed by an earthquake. Judith wrote about riding a horse around the walls of Jerusalem, and of visiting six different synagogues representing different Jewish traditions, including Ashkenzai and different forms of Sephardi Jewish heritages. On all their many travels, the Montefiores adhered to Jewish law, keeping kosher and Shabbat. They even traveled with their own *shochet* who slaughtered animals for them according to the rules of the Torah, ensuring that Judith and Moses always had access to the highest level of kosher foods.

Back home in England, Judith undertook a major writing project, though she kept it secret and it was years before she was revealed as the author. One of the first Jewish cookbooks, called *The Jewish Manual: or Practical Information in Jewish & Modern Cookery; with a Collection of Valuable Recipes and Hints Relating to the Toilette* was published in 1846. The author was described only as "A Lady"; historians now believe that Judith was the author. The book champions the values that Judith lived by: she recommends simplicity in dress, an attitude of giving charity and being kind, and a strict adherence to Jewish dietary law. Traditional English dishes were adapted for the kosher kitchen, replacing non-kosher ingredients such as lard or shellfish with kosher alternatives.

On the first evening of Rosh Hashanah in 1862, Judith was at home with Moses. They ate a festive Rosh Hashanah dinner together, and as Moses later recalled, the couple gave blessings to each other. After that, they went to bed. Sadly, Judith never woke up; she died peacefully in her sleep, after years of illnesses. She was mourned throughout the Jewish world.

Moses built a tomb for her in Ramsgate, in southern England, copying the design exactly from Rachel's Tomb near Jerusalem, where Judith had prayed so many years ago. He also established a Jewish school nearby, called the Judith Lady Montefiore College. Moses lived until the age of 101; when he passed away in 1885, he too was buried in Ramsgate near his wife. A few months before his death, he made one last bequest: additional funds to be used to maintain Rachel's Tomb in the Land of Israel, where he and Judith had spent some of their most important and informative times, praying to God and immersed in helping their fellow Jews.

Hannah Rochel Werbermacher (Maid of Ludomir)
c1806 - c1888

Mea Shearim, Jerusalem

She's inspired numerous books and plays, including Isaac Bashevis Singer's novel *Shosha*. The key events and dates of her life vary according to who is telling her story. "She was a riddle in life and in death, and so she remains until today," noted historian Samuel Horodezky.

Yet in her long life, Hannah Rochel Werbermacher influenced countless Jews, teaching and inspiring them with her own intense religious fervor and sharing her knowledge and love of Torah. Like a stone thrown into a river, the ripples she created still move today. Many of the details of her life have been lost to history, but we continue to hear echoes of her vivid life.

Hannah was born in the town of Ludomir, in Ukraine: many biographers cite 1815 as her birth year, though her biographer Nathaniel Deutsch dates her birth to 1806. In the generation still remembered by Hannah's grandparents, Ludomir's Jews were devastated by the Chmielnicki Uprising: a Cossack rebellion between 1648-1649 in which Jews were targeted and up to half a million Jews across Ukraine were murdered. By 1662, Ludomir's Jewish population had been cut to a mere

318. The community began to rebuild, and by 1765 the census recorded 159 Jewish households in the town.

At the time, Hasidism was sweeping through Jewish communities in the region. Drawing on Jewish mysticism, Chassidim (meaning "pious people") sought a visceral connection with the Divine through singing, dancing and intense prayer. Chassidic Rebbes gained popularity, leading small communities in prayer and study, serving as spiritual guides, and forging intensely personal connections with their followers. In 1786 the distinguished Chassidic rebbe Rabbi Shelomoh ha-Levi settled in the town and turned Ludomir into a major Chassidic center; he was murdered in 1792 in a crime that surely traumatized Ludomir's small Jewish community.

Hannah's family was likely not Chassidic, and they were also unusual in being relatively wealthy: her father, Reb Monesh Verbermacher was a well-to-do merchant. Hannah was a talented and intensely religious child: at an early age she became a scholar of Jewish texts, including the Talmud. Even though it was the custom at the time (and today as well) for Orthodox Jewish men to pray three times a day and for women to pray less often - usually once or twice a day instead - Hannah insisted on praying three times a day, reciting the Morning, Afternoon and Evening Jewish services. Some say that she wore a tallis and tefillin like a man.

When she was a teenager, tragedy struck: Hannah's mother became ill and died. Many accounts of Hannah's life mention that around the same time, she became engaged to a young man with whom she was deeply in love, and somehow their plans to marry were thwarted. All agree that Hannah fell into a deep depression: she rarely left her home, and only then to visit her mother's grave. One day, Hannah fell asleep at the grave. (Some say she was running and tripped and was knocked unconscious.) When she awoke, a great change had occurred. Hannah announced to her father that in her dreams, she approached the Heavenly Court, and was granted an additional, elevated soul.

When Hannah's father passed away some years later, she inherited a large sum of money and bought the upper story of a building in Ludomir, which she turned into a synagogue called the *gornshtibl* (the "upper level" shtiebel, or small synagogue.)

Hannah acted much like the Chassidic rebbes of the day, providing spiritual guidance and a space for a tight-knit community to flourish and leading prayers. Each Shabbat, Hannah led a *tish*, a Friday night gathering featuring divrei Torah, food and singing. This was a major hallmark of the role of a Chassidic rebbe. Hannah would teach Torah from behind a screen in order to protect her modesty.

She garnered intense personal loyalty and veneration. It's said that she performed healings on local Jews. (In this, it seems that she was acting in a traditional female capacity: *apshprecherkes* were traditional Jewish faith healers, often women.) Soon, a group of mostly poor local men and women were her followers: some called her the Maiden of Ludomir, and those who venerated her were known (possibly ironically) as the Maid of Ludomir's "Chassidim".

The "Maid of Ludomir" aroused no small amount of opprobrium. Even though Jewish communities in Eastern Europe had female leadership figures - *fizogerin*, for instance, led prayers in the women's galleries of synagogues - Hannah Rochel Webermacher was crossing some inviolate gender norms. Some said she was possessed by a dybbuk, or spirit. Eventually, Hannah's detractors appealed to the greatest Chassidic leader in the area for assistance, asking Rabbi Mordechai Twersky, known as the Maggid of Chernobyl, to help.

Rabbi Twersky met with Hannah and pressured her to marry. She did so, but it seems that her husband was too in awe of her as a holy woman to consummate the marriage: they divorced soon after. Her disastrous marriage seems to have been a turning point for Hannah and her influence began to wane, whether - as some accounts say - she lost her special spiritual powers after her divorce - or perhaps she no longer commanded the same mysterious respect.

Around the year 1860, Hannah moved to Israel and re-established herself as a Jewish leader there, setting up her own synagogue first in the Old City of Jerusalem and later moving to the new Jewish settlement of Mea Shearim. She was generally considered a member of the local Volhynian Chassidic community (Volhynia being the region in Ukraine where Ludomir sits). Yet her appeal went far beyond the community of her origin.

In Jerusalem, Hannah once again taught Torah and provided spiritual guidance; before long, the Maid of Ludomir had built another circle of followers in the Holy Land. This time, her students included Chassidic women and some men, Sephardi Jews, and even some Muslim Arab women who were drawn to her intense spirituality and uplifting lessons. It seems she led prayers and taught Torah in her own synagogue once more. She also led prayer groups to daaven (pray) at the Western Wall and the Tomb of the Matriarch Rachel near Jerusalem.

Hannah passed away in Jerusalem sometime around 1888 and was buried on the Mount of Olives. Legend says that a large procession accompanied her to her final resting place. Her biographer Nathaniel Deutsch has combed newspaper records from the era and failed to find any mention of such a great funeral procession. He posits that this might have been because by the time of her death, Hannah was in failing health and no longer the towering teacher she was in her youth. It could also be "that because her followers were largely poor and working-class women she was not perceived as an important figure by the male editors" of the newspapers of the day.

Long neglected, her gravestone was destroyed by Jordanian forces who controlled much of Jerusalem from 1948-1967. In 2004, a small group of local Jerusalem feminists led a campaign to install a new tombstone on Hannah's grave, once again marking the final resting place of this remarkable, restless and intensely religious Jewish leader.

Solica Hatchouel
1817-1834

Each year, both Jewish and Muslim pilgrims make their way to the old Jewish cemetery in Fez, the renown city in northern Morocco, where generations of Jews once lived, forming one of North Africa's most vibrant Jewish communities. They visit on the *hilloula* - Aramaic for the Hebrew word *yahrzeit*, or anniversary of a death - of Rabbi Chaim Ha'Cohen (1836-1924), a local sage of great renown.

His *hilloula* serves as the unofficial date of when another Jew buried in the cemetery nearby is honored too: a Jewish teenage girl named Solica (also spelled Soulika or Sol, and sometimes known as Soulika Ha'Tzadekkes - or Soulika the Righteous Woman). According to one legend, only her head is buried in the cemetery, testament to the horrible, violent way she died.

Many of the details of Solica's life and death are lost to history. Her story has been told and retold: it's the subject of melancholy ballads in French, Spanish, Arabic and Hebrew, each of which present their own version of her tale. Books, plays and at least one movie have been made about her. The great French artist Alfred Dehodencq painted several versions of Solica in the midst of her torment, including the picture at the beginning of this chapter. Historian Sharon Vance, who wrote one of the few rigorously academic analyses of Solica Hatchouel has explained that "It is impossible to do a thorough study of all the written and oral works devoted to Sol, particularly given the fact that her story continues to be retold in both written and oral form and is an ongoing tradition that generates new texts."

Yet a few facts are clear, forming a common thread through the many differing descriptions of the life and death of this remarkable young Jewish woman. Solica was born in 1817 to a middle-class Jewish family in Tangier. Her parents Chaim and Simcha were simple and pious: Chaim opened the family's modest home to Jewish study groups. Solica grew up steeped in religious values, yet sadly peace seemingly eluded her home.

These bare facts were recorded by Eugenio Maria Romero, a Spanish traveler who met one of Solica's brothers in Gibraltar soon after her death. Romero was shocked and fascinated by the tragic tale, and visited Tangier in Morocco in order to meet with Solica's relatives, including her heartbroken parents. After returning to Gibraltar, he wrote an account of her death titled *El Martirio de la joven Hachuel o la Heroina Hebrea*, "The Martyrdom of the Young Hatchouel, or The Jewish Heroine". It was published in Spain in 1837, just three years after Solica's murder.

A second version of Solica's sad tale was published in France in 1844 by a French traveler known only as M. Rey. He too described speaking with Solica's brothers; his book *Souvenirs d'un Voyage au Maroc*, or Memories of a Trip to Morocco, provides an account of Solica's travails that largely accords with Romero's book.

According to both accounts, Solica and her mother had a strained relationship, fighting bitterly over anything and everything. Solica's mother Simcha was a hard taskmaster: the family had no servants, and Simcha would berate Solica for not doing a better job with her many household chores.

Tangier was distinctive among Moroccan towns for having no special Jewish Quarter: Jews and Muslims sometimes found themselves neighbors, and this was the case with the Hatchouel family. Solica became close with a young Muslim woman named Tahra de Mesmudi, whose house seemingly shared a courtyard with the Hatchouels. Solica would find refuge there after particularly unpleasant fights with her mother. Tahra often suggested to Solica that she convert to Islam. Solica would deflect these suggestions and the two girls managed to remain staunch friends despite their differences in religion and Tahra's missionary pressures.

After one particularly vicious fight with her mother over housework, Solica fled once again to Tahra's house, where she cried in her friend's arms and tearfully declared that she wished she could leave her own family home forever. Tragically, this outburst seems to have led Tahra to take drastic measures. When Solica's story is told by Muslim writers, at this point they declare that Solica embraced Islam and converted with Tahra's aid. Jewish renditions of this story say that Solica resisted Tahra's entreaties to convert. The two accounts that were written in the immediate aftermath of Solica's death, after the authors spoke with her relatives, maintain that Solica refused to abandon her Jewish faith.

While Solica stayed with Tahra's family, Tahra sent word to a local official named Arbi Esibo that a Jewish teenage girl was staying in her family's home and had consented to convert to Islam. Esibo sent for Solica and, against all custom, had her brought into his private chambers, not his official offices. Esibo kept Solica there, apparently asking her to convert and to marry a man of his choosing, yet she refused. According to M. Rey's account, word leaked out that the official was forcibly holding a young Jewish woman in his home. Within weeks, Sultan Abd al-Rahman of Morocco, a strong administrator and ardent champion of Islam, found out about the irregular situation and ordered Solica to be brought to the royal court in Fez.

When she was imprisoned in Esibo's home, Solica's family was able to smuggle food and news to her. Now, royal officials forbade all contact. Solica's father, Chaim, was told to pay an exorbitant fee to cover the expenses of his daughter's forced conveyance to Fez, or else face 500 lashes. He borrowed the money from Spain's Vice-Consul in Morocco, and paid an additional amount to a Jew to follow Solica to Fez and report back on her condition.

The day of her conveyance, Solica was released from Esibo's house looking pale, with heavy chains around her ankles. She was tied to a donkey and spent six agonizing days on the long journey to Fez. Once there, she was greeted by a huge display of soldiers, and sent to the Sultan's personal harem. Solica refused all efforts to convert her, including during a fateful meeting with the Sultan himself, during which he presented the Jewish teenager with a brutal choice: convert and accept a royal marriage with a man of the Sultan's choosing, or die. Solica bravely answered that she would prefer death.

Some accounts of what happened next assert that the Sultan called for the greatest rabbis of Fez to come and persuade Solica to convert to Islam, and that the rabbis did tell Solica to convert. These accounts stress that the Sultan threatened violence and ruin on the entire Jewish community if Solica refused to convert to Islam. Other accounts say that Jewish sages and other members of Fez's Jewish community did visit Solica, but to console her.

Finally, the order came: if she continued to cling to her Jewish faith, Solica would be beheaded. In Eugenio Maria Romero's telling, the executioner entered Solica's chamber with a trembling step: he'd seen the beautiful Jewish maiden and was devastated at the thought of her death. "Do you know the purpose of my coming?" he asked. "I know it," Solica replied. The executioner asked her one last time to leave her Jewish faith, and she refused, demanding instead to be led outside to the place of her execution. (Romero's book became a popular play within a few years of his writing, and it's easy to see how his artistic license would have ensured the story's dramatic tension.)

Whatever their actual conversation, decapitation was the Sultan's decree. It was a messy, horrific execution. A crowd circled round to watch Solica's death, with many screaming anti-Jewish slurs and calling for Solica's speedy murder. She first washed her hands in the Jewish ritual manner, then knelt, and said the *Shema Yisrael*, the last prayer Jews are meant to say before death.

The first blow to Solica's neck wasn't fatal. After delivering it, the executioner asked her one more time to convert to Islam, and one last time, Solica reaffirmed her commitment to remain Jewish. Only then did the final blow extinguish her life.

Fez's Jewish community managed to retrieve Solica's body to bury in the Jewish cemetery there. The Jewish sage Joseph Ben Naim wrote an account of how this was accomplished in 1835, a year after Solica's death. "Thick (clouds in the) sky flowed, strong rains, and gloom covered the face of the city, and even this did not dampen the anger of the Gentiles. They surrounded us like bees...and they wanted diligently to destroy her. From here and there came the cry to burn her body, as if they found a way to destroy the soul as well as the body. The sage Rabbi Raphael Ha'Aarfati mustered courage and strength and threw gold and gave bribes to the important people at court to rescue her body."

Bribed officials threw silver coins all over the ground so that "the fanatics and criminals" that had watched Solica's execution were distracted, scrambling in the mud for money. When Solica's mutilated body was finally brought to the gates of the Jewish quarter, the officials found that the gates had been closed, locking Fez's Jewish community into its cramped quarter. Rabbis and sages quickly managed to lift Solica's body over the walls, and brought her to the Jewish cemetery, terrified all the while that they would be spotted and set upon by the enraged crowd.

"Wali (what a great misfortune for me) over what happened...to this virgin. I will cry and moan for that which happened...nothing like it has happened in my time," wrote Moshe Ben Sa'adon, a Jewish poet of Fez shortly after Solica's murder.

In time, legends sprung up that praying at Solica's grave could bring about miracles. She was seen as a protector of children, Jews and Muslims alike named daughters after her, supposedly as a way of gaining good luck and receiving the blessings of Solica's righteousness. Her tomb is adorned with inscriptions in two languages, French and Hebrew. Her French epitaph reads "Here lies Miss Solica Hatchouel, born in Tangier in 1817. Refusing to enter into the Islamic religion, Arabs assassinated her in Fez in 1834. Torn away from her family, the whole world mourns this saintly child."

The Hebrew inscription on Solica's grave employs terms that would likely have been more familiar to this religious, loyal, determined and desperately unhappy Jewish teenager: "The gravestone of the righteous Solica Hatchouel, a virgin maiden who greatly sanctified the Name of Heaven and died a martyr in the glorious city of Fez in the year 5594 (1834) and is buried here. May the Lord protect her. May her merit protect us. May it be God's will".

Devorah Romm
1831-1903

Every day thousands of Jews open the pages of the Talmud and pour over pages
that look remarkably similar. Most editions of the Talmud, no matter where they
are published, use a common format: a portion of text from the Mishnah and the
Gemara placed in the center of each page, surrounded by commentaries by rabbis.
Some additional commentaries are included at the bottom of each page and in the
back of each volume.

So widespread is this format that few people question its origins. The story of how
it came would be shocking if it weren't so little known: Devorah Romm is the
little-remembered printer who perfected the "Vilna Shas" edition of the Talmud
that today is the default Talmudic layout around the world. She worked at a time

when it was unheard of for women to study the Talmud, yet her erudition and scholarly attention to detail is present on every page.

Only some details are known about Devorah's early life: she was born in 1831 in Novagroduk, a bustling town of several thousand people, a majority of whom were Jews, in today's Belarus. Her father, Rabbi Bezaleel Harkavy, taught Devorah Hebrew, Talmud, and Torah: she spoke five languages and was more highly educated in Jewish subjects than many women in her day.

Devorah moved to Vilna and married David Romm, a scion of the famous Romm Jewish book publishing dynasty. It's not difficult to imagine these two erudite, highly educated scholars debating the finer points of Jewish books in their free hours together. By the mid-1800s, the Romm publishing house enjoyed a renowned reputation and David Romm was a major force behind the flourishing of Jewish scholarship that earned Vilna in the 1800s the moniker the "Jerusalem" of Lithuania.

Dating from 1789, when it opened in the Belarusian town of Grodno, the Romm family press opened a second printing house in 1799 in Vilna, in Lithuania, which was a major center of Jewish erudition.

From the beginning, the Romm company's output was different from other presses. In Vilna, the company's second-generation owner, Menachem Romm, hired a gifted engraver named Rabbi Lipman Metz to create an entirely new Hebrew font: Rabbi Metz's creation is known as the Vilna font, and is still in use today. With brand new Hebrew printing plates creating books and pamphlets in a beautiful new style, the Romm press became the gold standard of Jewish book publishing in the region. Local government agencies even began to use the Romm family business to print official documents.

In 1834, the Romm family embarked on an ambitious novel project: creating a new, improved edition of the Talmud. They assembled a stellar committee of rabbis and some of Vilna's leading scholars, who worked for close to twenty years to proofread and set the extensive text. (With 63 masechtot, or tractates, the Babylonian Talmud - the edition that is most often studied - is a huge body of work, akin to a complete set of Encyclopedia in English.) The Romm edition was to include rabbinic commentaries that had not previously been printed in editions of the Talmud.

As Romm's team of scholars toiled on the project, other Jewish printing houses announced plans to publish similar editions of their own. Before long, intense rivalries and disputes about copyrighted work broke out. The discord was so acrimonious that it reached the court of Czar Nicholas I, who decided to intervene, disastrously for Jewish publishing. The Czar shut down all Jewish printing companies in the Russian Empire, with only two exceptions: one in Kiev and one in Vilna. Even more disastrously, Czar Nicholas I decreed that Jewish books could only be distributed in a small area.

The Romm press was granted the Czar's permission to be the sole Jewish printing house in all of Lithuania, but at a crushing cost. They had to cooperate with heavy government censorship, and under the new law, Romm's books could no longer be sold in Poland, which was home to some of the largest Jewish communities in the world. Schools and individuals which had pre-ordered the Romm edition of the Talmud canceled their orders, threatening the company with utter ruin. Romm held on, but only just. Their long-awaited edition of the Talmud came out in 1854, finally allowing the company to regain a sound financial footing.

David Romm took over the firm in 1858, along with his two younger brothers. With Devorah's help, David started planning an even more ambitious new edition of the Talmud, but sadly he was never able to see the new edition of which he and Devorah had dreamed.

Devorah Romm was home in Vilna with her six young children in 1862 when she got the news: her husband David had suffered a heart attack while on a business trip to St. Petersburg. A widow at age 31 with a large family, Devorah decided to take over her husband's business role and shepherd a new, even more impressive, Romm edition of the Talmud to completion.

The company changed its title pages to read *Defus ha'Almanah v'ha'Achim Romm* - the Press of the Widow and the Brothers Romm. Devorah became widely known as *ha'Almanah Romm*, "the Widow Romm," and commanded great respect in the publishing world. Firmly in charge of the press, she instituted four immediate reforms.

One was investing heavily in the new invention of stereotypes, whole sheets of set type that allowed printers to print multiple copies of books more quickly and inexpensively. She also improved the quality of her company's editing - typos were a common problem in Jewish books - and took pains to keep printing projects away from the government censor, whose interference had lowered the quality of their work. Finally, she paid more attention to the aesthetics of the company's books, improving the layout and making sure that books looked attractive and clean.

The first book *ha'Almanah Romm* - the Widow Romm - published was a *siddur*, a Jewish prayer book, which showcased the results of the changes Devorah had made. The *siddur* was a runaway success, selling hundreds of thousands of copies, and burnishing Devorah's reputation. She next turned to the longstanding plan of publishing yet another edition of the Talmud, even more attractive, innovative and complete than the company's previous product.

Given the huge expense involved, many of Devorah's friends tried to convince her to abandon her plan. Hiring another army of scholars would be too big an undertaking, it was thought. Devorah and her brothers-in-law came up with a plan: they put together a few sample pages and sent out circulars to potential customers describing their endeavor and asking for prepaid orders. Devorah thought that if 4,000 customers pre-ordered a set of Talmud, she could pay for the project. To her surprise, over 10,000 orders came in. Devorah got to work on a monumental edition of *Shas*, as the complete set of Talmud is called. She hired a large staff of Jewish scholars, helping support a number of rabbis and sustain Jewish life in Vilna.

Devorah's new edition of the Talmud would include previously unpublished rabbinic commentaries on the text. One of the most eagerly anticipated was that of Rabbenu Chananel (965-1055), the first scholar to write a complete commentary on the Talmud. Rabbenu Chananel headed a major rabbinic academy in modern-day Tunisia. Many of his writings have been lost to history: obtaining even a portion of new commentary would be a major achievement. Devorah was determined to do all she could to include his words in her work.

The only known copies of some of Rabbenu Chananel's key commentaries were located in the Vatican's Apostolic Archive (known until 2019 as the "Vatican Secret Archive") in Rome. They were virtually impossible to access until 1878, when Leo XIII became Pope and moved to open the Archives to researchers. Devorah sent a team of researchers to Rome to decipher and transcribe Rabbenu Chananel's words. Their task was made even more difficult by the poor condition of the Archives documents and by the fact that the only known copies of the commentary had been translated into Latin: it took months for Devorah's scholars to decipher them and translate them back into Hebrew.

Devorah's researchers stayed in Rome for months. When the Archives announced they were closing for their long Summer holiday, Devorah appealed directly to Cardinal Joseph Hergenrother, the first Cardinal-Prefect of the newly opened Archives. He kept the Archives open just for her team, on the condition that she pay a large fee for a private guard to ensure the security of the Archives during the long break. It was an offer Devorah eagerly accepted.

One of the workers on the project later recalled the feeling of excitement that he and other scholars in Devorah's employ felt. "Looking in retrospect, the Vatican had always been the source of deadly hatred of the Jewish nation and even more so of our literature, (hatred) that spread to every Christian land, often leading kings to level decrees of forced apostasy, slaughter, killing, destruction and harsh exile…Worst of all, they confiscated and burned Jewish books on many occasions, sometimes decreeing that the Jew be burned together with the holy books…Now, wonder of wonders, out of the very furnace into which they always threw Jewish books for burning, kindness and goodwill that are unparalleled even towards Christian rulers…are being extended towards those very same" holy Jewish books. It was a historic moment, made possible by Devorah Romm's determination.

Finally, in 1886, Devorah unveiled the edition of the Talmud known today as the Vilna Shas. It was a masterful work, containing over a hundred commentaries, some of which had never been published before. It radiated careful proofreading, scholarship, editing and printing, and was an instant success, soon becoming the standard model of Talmud the world over.

Devorah Romm died in 1903, a beloved fixture in Vilna, the city whose Jewish life she'd done so much to support and enrich. Without her leadership, the Romm press declined. Once one of the largest Jewish-owned companies in the world, it became a shadow of its former self. In 1940, it passed into Soviet hands and became a government printing house. Yet in the depths of the Holocaust, the Romm press did the Jewish people one more service.

When Nazi forces entered Vilna in 1941, they interred local Jews in two infamous Vilna Ghettos. From there, over 50,000 Jews were deported to Nazi death camps or brought to a nearby forest and shot. Yet Jews resisted; in 1942, a group of young fighters formed a partisan resistance group inside the Vilna Ghettos. One of these young fighters was the poet Avrom Sutzkever, who helped build Jewish defenses, even melting down metal which he formed into bullets. One night, he snuck out of the Ghetto with another fighter and made his way down darkened streets to the old Romm printing company: there they stole metal plates from the presses which were given new life as Sutzkever melted them down to form into bullets. Sutzkever later wrote a haunting poem "The Lead Plates at the Romm Press" about that night.

Arrayed at night, like fingers stretch through bars
To clutch the lit air of freedom,
We made for the press plates, to seize
The lead plates at the Romm printing works.....

...So, pouring out line after lettered line, did we
Letter by melting letter the lead,
Liquified bullets, gleamed with thoughts:
A verse from Babylon, a verse from Poland,
Seething, flowing into the one mold...

(Translated by Neal Kozodoy)

Sutzkever's poem was widely circulated at the time, lending strength and hope to those terrified Jews who read his words. His description of the Romm press sustaining Jewish life was powerful then, and it is apt today too. The Romm press helped Jews physically survive in 1942. It helped us spiritually flourish during the glory days of the 19th Century when Vilna was indeed the "Jerusalem of Lithuania". It continues to sustain us still: the books that Devorah Romm and her family published there, the definitive version of the Talmud that she created, continue to be read, to be studied and loved, and nourish Jewish souls across the globe today.

Hannah Sandusky
1837 - 1913

For thousands of Jews living around the turn of the century in Pittsburgh, she was known as the "Angel" and the "Saint." Her name was Hannah Sandusky, and in later life she was also known as Bubbe (Grandma) Hannah. She was one of Pittsburgh's most successful midwives, working predominantly in the city's working-class Hill District for decades. Bubbe Hannah delivered thousands of children and ministered to poor immigrant and Black women who were often marginalized and forgotten by the mainstream medical establishment.

She used to wear a black bonnet and cape, and always had a pocket full of candy for the local children. "My mother told me that when I saw Bobba Hannah I should run and make hot coffee because she was our honored guest," explained former Pittsburgh resident Etta Meyers Katz, in an interview with the historian Ida Selevan years later.

"Bubbe Hannah" was born in 1827 in the town of Kovno, Lithuania, which was home to a thriving and learned Jewish community. Her mother was a midwife, and Hannah learned how to assist during births from her. Hannah married a glazier named Louis Sandusky and they emigrated to Pittsburgh in 1861. That was the year the American Civil War began, and Pittsburgh's Jewish community responded to the crisis by setting up a vibrant charitable network to aid the war effort. Many of these Jews were recent immigrants, but they worked to defend their new homeland, raising money for the Union war effort, sewing clothes and providing aid to Union soldiers and their families. When the war ended in 1865, many of the Jewish women in Pittsburgh decided to continue their charitable work, and formed the Hebrew Ladies Aid Society, the city's first official Jewish charitable organization. The Society arranged for visits to the sick and raised money to buy necessities for poor families. Hannah was an early volunteer, and worked as a nurse and midwife.

A fervently religious woman, Hannah also worked within Pittsburgh's Orthodox community. She and Louis helped found Congregation Beth Hamedrash Hagodol, and Hannah volunteered her time making shrouds for the local Jewish burial society, consoling mourners, sewing brides' wedding trousseaus, and working as a matchmaker. The couple had seven children. Despite her overwhelmingly busy home life, Hannah also maintained a busy schedule attending births. She gained a sterling reputation as a first rate midwife, and was soon being called in regularly by a local doctor whenever he faced a particularly difficult delivery. This doctor would invite his peers to births that Hannah attended, instructing them that they could learn from this Jewish immigrant woman.

When one of Hannah's sons developed an eye disease, the doctor she assisted paid for her to take him to a famous eye specialist in Germany. While her son was undergoing medical treatment in Germany, Hannah formally studied nursing and midwifery, becoming a qualified midwife. After a year in Germany, Hannah and her son returned to Pittsburgh; at the time, Hannah was one of the few officially licensed midwives in all of the United States. She set up a practice in the Hill District, tending to the poor Jewish immigrants who were pouring into Pittsburgh from Eastern Europe, and also working with the Black community, who were largely shunned by the white medical professionals at the time. In all her long years of practicing medicine, she never charged for her services.

As she grew older, her fame increased and "Bubbe Hannah" became a beloved fixture in the District. The City of Pittsburgh only began keeping records of births in 1870: according to official accounts, Hannah delivered 3,571 babies. Her great grandchildren believe the true number was far higher. She delivered her final baby in 1909, at the age of 82.

In 2010, Hannah's descendents endowed the "Bubbe Hannah Fund" at a Midwife Center in Pittsburgh, aiding under-insured pregnant women in the city who are at risk of poor health outcomes. It was a fitting honor in memory of this uniquely selfless, pious Jewish woman who dedicated her all, throughout her long life, to helping her fellow women.

Emma Lazarus
1849 - 1887

In 1886, France donated a massive gift to the United States: a 305-foot tall statue of a woman holding a torch aloft, symbolizing the shared love of liberty in both nations. But there was one problem: there was no place to display such a towering statue.

Arts lovers in New York scrambled to raise money to erect a platform for the new statue on Ellis Island in New York Harbor. Hoping to raise publicity and funds, they turned to Emma Lazarus, one of the nation's best-known poets, beseeching her to write a poem about the statue. Emma initially was resistant, but then gave in, hoping to raise awareness for the plight of poor Jews and other refugees. Her poem *The New Colossus*, including its iconic plea "Give me your tired, your poor, your huddled masses yearning to breathe free", was eventually carved into the base of the Statue of Liberty.

Emma Lazarus started off life with little formal connection to the Jewish community. Born in 1849 into an assimilated Jewish family, Emma's parents Moses and Esther traced their lineage back to some of America's earliest Sephardi Jewish settlers from Spain and Portugal, but the family wasn't particularly observant. Moses Lazarus was a successful sugar trader and the family lived in a comfortable house near New York's Union Square Park. Emma grew up with a sound classical education, fluent in French and German. Most of her friends were Christian.

Nevertheless, Emma was intensely proud of her noble Jewish ancestors and often wrote about the Jewish rabbis and poets in Spain's Golden Age, before the expulsion of Jews from Spain in 1492. As a child, Emma showed early promise as a poet and her father encouraged her, publishing her first book of poems and encouraging Emma to meet and correspond with America's leading literary figures. She became a fixture in New York literary society and traveled extensively in Europe, counting Ralph Waldo Emerson, Robert Browning, Henry James and William Morris as friends. She once wrote home that she was "drinking in with every sense the spirit...and the beauty of life."

Though she lived largely in non-Jewish society, Emma was aware that she was sometimes the target of anti-Semitic comments behind her back. "I am perfectly conscious that this contempt and hatred underlies the general tone of the community towards us, and yet when I even remotely hint at the fact that we are not a favorite people I am accused of stirring up strife and setting barriers...." she wrote to her friend and literary journalist Philip Cowen in 1883.

A series of bloody pogroms in Eastern Europe in the 1880s sent Jews scrambling to find refuge in America. Between 1881 and 1898 over half a million Jews moved to the United States. These immigrants were as different from the refined, assimilated Jewish community of Emma Lazarus' youth as could be. They were, for the most part, Ashkenazi, more religiously observant, and had fled with very few possessions. As New York's Jewish population grew, so did anti-Semitism. Emma was appalled at the hostility shown to her co-religionists and began to advocate for them, defying expectations of how a refined young lady should behave.

Emma had previously translated poems by the great German Jewish poet Heinrich Heine, and now she began to identify with his brand of political activism, wielding her pen as a weapon for truth. Though Heine hadn't been religiously observant, Emma wrote, "he was none the less eager to proclaim himself an enthusiast for the rights of the Jews..." Increasingly, so was she.

Emma translated into English some German translations of Medieval Hebrew poetry, bringing these beautiful Jewish works to an American audience for the first time. In 1882 she published a book, *Songs of a Semite*, that dealt with Jewish themes. Later that year she wrote a play about Jewish persecution in Medieval Germany. Emma wrote an impassioned essay about Henry Wadsworth Longfellow's celebrated poem *The Jewish Cemetery at Newport*, taking strong exception to Longfellow's final line, "dead nations never rise again." Nonsense, wrote Emma Lazarus, the many Jews coming to America "prove them to be very warmly and thoroughly alive."

That life was increasingly visible to Emma Lazarus as she got to know the new Jewish immigrants in New York. She visited impoverished neighborhoods, volunteered with the Hebrew Immigrant Aid Society, and helped found the Hebrew Technical Institute to teach needy Jews job skills. "What would my society friends say if they saw me here?" Emma sometimes joked.

Emma began to call for a Jewish homeland in Israel. In 1882, 15 years before the first Zionist Congress in Zurich, she penned a series of open letters in the journal *American Hebrew*, called "Epistle to the Hebrews," calling for American Jews to help establish a Jewish state.

Her series would eventually grow to a set of fifteen missives, spanning two years, that eloquently issued a call to action. Explaining to Jewish middle class readers what was happening to their fellow Jews abroad, Emma urged: "We who are prosperous and independent" should feel solidarity with Jews the world over. "Until we are all free, we are none of us free."

At the end of 1882, when she was in the midst of penning her open letters, Emma wrote *The New Year (Rosh Hashanah, 5643)*, an influential poem that beautifully conveyed her vision of a people "rolling homeward to its ancient source."

Emma was ahead of her time. She died in 1887 at the age of 38, ten years before Theodore Herzl echoed her call for a Jewish homeland at the Zionist Congress. Twenty years after it first appeared, her Epistle to the Hebrews was reprinted by the Zionist Federation of America. American Zionist leader Henrietta Szold credited Emma with helping spark the Zionist movement: "With her own hand she has sown the seeds that shall transform her grave into a garden."

Emma Lazarus' best known poem, *The New Colossus*, was not displayed in her lifetime. Only in 1903 was it finally engraved on the base of the Statue of Liberty in New York Harbor. By then, foes of immigration were calling for fewer Jews in the United States. In 1924, the Johnson-Reed Act severely limited the number of Jews who could find refuge in the United States; only about 200,000 Jews were admitted to the country from 1933 to 1945. Emma Lazarus' dream of a Jewish refuge went unheeded.

In 1948, however, Emma Lazarus' dream of a new Jewish homeland came true, with the establishment of the State of Israel, nearly seven decades after she first bravely called for the return of her ancient people to its source.

Farha Sassoon
1856 - 1936

In 1856, the year Farha Sassoon was born, the Indian city of Mumbai was a bustling, growing home to diverse Jewish communities.

Bene Israel Jews, who traced their presence in India to an ancient shipwreck which deposited a Jewish community on India's shores, began migrating to Mumbai in the late 1700s, building synagogues and other civic institutions. Other Jews from Yemen, Afghanistan, Iran and Bukhara later poured into the city, drawn by its rapidly expanding business opportunities. Yet nobody electrified Mumbai's Jewish community as much as David Sassoon, Farha's great grandfather. He moved to India in 1832 to escape rising persecution from local rulers in his native Iraq, and founded the trading company David Sassoon & Co. in his new home.

One observer summed up the business: "Silver and gold, silks, gums and spices, opium, cotton wool and wheat - whatever moved over land and sea felt the hand and bore the mark of Sassoon and Company." David developed Mumbai's Sassoon Docks, and before long opened company branches throughout India, China, Hong Kong, Japan, Iraq and Britain, sending his sons to various locales to oversee their businesses there. Some likened the Sassoon family to the Rothschilds, another Jewish family with business interests spanning many countries, bestowing the moniker "the Rothschilds of the East." A devout Jew, David Sassoon also built synagogues, Jewish hospitals and schools across Mumbai and beyond, electrifying India's Jewish community. Farha was his great-granddaughter.

Like many other Mumbai Jews, Farha spoke Hindi and English outside her home, and Judeo-Arabic with her relatives. At the time, Mumbai Jews competed in business with the Parsees, Zoroastrians who fled from Persia to India in the 7th and 8th Centuries. Jews began to copy the Parsee tradition of educating their sons but not their daughters. For Farha's parents, however, failing to teach their brilliant daughter was not an option. Farha attended a Catholic school in Mumbai, and her parents hired rabbis from Baghdad to tutor her and her siblings in the evenings. She became fluent in Hebrew, Aramaic (the language of the Talmud), Hindi, English, French and German.

Farha married David Solomon's youngest son Shlomo in 1876. Twenty-eight years her senior, Shlomo was also her great-uncle. Despite its unconventionality, the marriage seems to have been happy. Both Farha and Shlomo were intensely religious, quick-witted and hard-working, and they operated together as a team in both the realm of business and in their private philanthropic work. They had three children together - David Solomon, Rachel and Mozelle - and spent much of their time in their magnificent country house outside of Mumbai in the town of Pune, where Farha and Solomon spent much of their time studying Jewish texts.

Friends noted that Farha adored her husband for his piety and modesty. When he entered the synagogue he'd founded in Mumbai, it's said that Solomon would quietly slip in through a side door so as not to attract attention to himself. Farha and Solomon were extremely wealthy and occupied the highest rungs of the British Empire's social structure; the Prince of Wales even dined at their house in Pune. Yet while she could entertain in the highest of style, Farha kept a strictly kosher kitchen and encouraged her guests to try the myriad different delicacies she served. (Years later, the Prince of Wales still talked about the gifts of amba - a pickled mango relish which is popular in Mizrahi Jewish cooking - and dried apricots which Farha gave him.)

When Solomon traveled to their home in Mumbai for business, Farha broke all taboos on women's roles and accompanied him to the city's financial district in Elphinstone Circle, sitting in on business meetings and acting as an active partner in the family company. At the time, it was a shocking assertion of independence. Despite some misgivings in Mumbai's business community, Farha eventually was accepted as a fully-fledged manager within David Solomon & Co.

Her position stood her in good stead in 1894, when Solomon suddenly passed away. Farha declared that she was ready to take Solomon's place. Biographer Joseph Sassoon notes: the "Sassoon family was not prepared for a female leader. They couldn't look to the old country and Baghdad for a precedent, and though seemingly every day brought news of the suffragettes' activities in England, women did not run global companies there either." Yet after extensive discussion, it was finally agreed: Farha Sassoon would take over the running of David Sassoon and Co.'s operations in Mumbai, as a full partner. With Farha at the helm, the company weathered a number of storms, including the outbreak of the First Sino-Japanese War and falling commodity prices. Despite the difficult business environment, the Mumbai office's profits rose during Farha's leadership.

Business was only one of Farha's occupations. A vigorous woman in her late 30s when she became leader of the company's Indian branch, Farha was a hands-on parent to her three children; letters show her arranging playdates and arranging for her son to take a boat tour of the East accompanied by servants and "a small stock of live fowls on board…to keep kosher while aboard." Farha's daughter Mozelle had been dropped by a nurse when she was an infant and suffered from spinal injuries her whole life. Farha doted on her, making sure Mozelle was looked after, and also tutored her - and her other children - in Jewish studies. Farha threw herself into improving her homeland. She campaigned against the practice of purdah, according to which some Indian women hid themselves away from everyone but close family members. Farha also financially supported Waldemar Mordechai Wolff Haffkine, the Russian-born Jewish bacteriologist who set up a laboratory in the Byculla neighborhood of Mumbai, where he developed vaccines against cholera and the Bubonic plague.

Throughout her life, Farha kept up a busy correspondence with many of the most eminent rabbis of the age. In 2007, the Sassoon family published a book titled *Nahalat Avot* (Heritage of our Forefathers), comprising the many letters by great Torah sages that were sent to the Sassoon family. A large proportion of them were sent to Farha. Surprisingly, many of them referred to Farha as "Rabbanit," a term that is used today to denote a learned woman in the Orthodox tradition, but one that was virtually unheard of in the 1800s.

In 1901, shifting alliances within David Sassoon & Co. forced Farha out of her chairmanship role. Many of her relatives had moved from Mumbai to London, and Farha joined them there, hoping to obtain a higher level of medical care for Mozelle. She anglicized her name to Flora, and devoted herself entirely to Torah study and to entertaining on a grand scale. Few of the visitors to Farha's grand house at 32 Bruton Street in London's swanky Mayfair neighborhood realized that her legendary banquets were strictly kosher. She held open salons once a week where the cream of London's society would gather to speak with one another and to hear Farha's considered opinions on the matters of the day. The historian Cecil Roth said she "walked like a queen, talked like a sage and entertained like an Oriental potentate."

Farha had a strict policy of responding to letters on the same day they arrived. Jews all over the world appealed to her; many of the letters were simply addressed to "Flora Sassoon, England" - and somehow found their way to her. She donated money to help rebuild San Francisco after the devastating earthquake there in 1906, supported Jewish schools and charities, and bankrolled Jewish hospitals and orphanages in England and across the Middle East. With the rise of Nazism, Farha campaigned to support Jewish refugees applying to move to England. A staunch Zionist, Farha was outspoken in her support of establishing a Jewish state in the Land of Israel. She traveled widely, always bringing along an entourage of ten Jewish men so that she could pray with a minyan, as well as her own personal shochet (kosher slaughterer), ensuring that she could always access kosher food.

On one trip, to Baghdad in 1910, Farha met with the son of Chacham Yosef Chaim (1832- 1909), the renowned rabbi and Jewish scholar known as the Ben Ish Chai. While visiting his synagogue, Farha was asked to read publicly from a Torah scroll that had been donated by the Sassoon family, an honor that was highly unusual to proffer to a woman. Yet Farha Sassoon was no ordinary woman. At a time when female scholarship was circumscribed, she authored Jewish articles about Talmudic and Midrashic texts for *The Jewish Forum*, a scholarly publication in the United States. An article she wrote about the Medieval Jewish commentator Rashi included a learned discussion of his work, and also highlighted the many erudite female members of his family.

Soon after her arrival in England, Farha was invited to speak at Jew's College, London's premier rabbinical training school. In 1924 she was invited back to preside over Speech Day there, and gave a learned speech teeming with Talmudic references and inspiring lessons to the budding rabbis in the audience. Her speech was later published by Oxford University Press. When Farha died in 1936, Rabbi Yitzhak Halevi Herzog, the Chief Rabbi of the Land of Israel (and former Chief Rabbi of Ireland) noted that she had been "a living well of Torah, of piety, of wisdom, of goodness and charity, the staunchest loyalty to tradition, and out of her wonderful well Israel could draw in abundance noble incentives and lofty inspiration." Farha was buried on the Mount of Olives in Jerusalem, in a plot that she'd purchased on a visit to the Land of Israel years earlier.

Henrietta Szold
1860 - 1945

Israelis observe Family Day each year on the 30th of the Hebrew month of Shevat. Few realize the surprising reason why: 30th Shevat is the birthdate of Henrietta Szold, the founder of Hadassah and one of the great early Zionists.

A brilliant and celebrated woman, Henrietta's life was nonetheless filled with profound regrets. She was born in Baltimore, just before the outbreak of America's Civil War. One of her earliest memories was being held up to the window to watch the convoy bearing President Abraham Lincoln's funeral cortege. Her home was intensely intellectual and steeped in Reform Jewish debates and culture: each week, her parents entertained prominent figures in the Reform religious movement at Shabbat meals, debating issues in the movement and politics of the day.

Henrietta's father, Rabbi Benjamin Szold, and her mother Sophie, were immigrants from Hungary; they'd felt the anti-Jewish hatred that infused so much of their native Europe and were profoundly grateful for the freedoms in America. Rabbi Szold was the spiritual leader of Temple Oheb Shalom in Baltimore, and Henerietta and four of her sisters grew up with their father's synagogue as a second home. (Another three sisters died in infancy.) Henrietta recalled reciting the Gettysburg Address in the synagogue as a young child, the adored and coddled daughter of the congregation's leader.

Rabbi Szold taught Henrietta Hebrew, German and some Aramaic. She learned French on her own at school. When she graduated from high school at the top of her class, many of her teachers tried to encourage her to go on to one of the new women's colleges that were opening at the time. Yet Henrietta didn't want to leave home and stayed with her parents, acting as her father's assistant. She sometimes confided in her sisters that she was sorry to have been born a girl, and felt sure she could have achieved great things had she been a man.

It is poignant to read in her letters how stymied Henrietta felt as a woman, because even at an early age she accomplished a huge amount. Yet time and again in her early years, Henrietta found herself overlooked, at times even exploited and underappreciated by her peers.

When Henrietta was in her twenties, poor Jewish immigrants from Russia and elsewhere in eastern Europe began pouring into the United States, including to Baltimore. Henrietta volunteered with local Jewish charities to aid the immigrants, but she went much further than anyone else in the city in helping her fellow Jews. In 1888, she founded the Russian Night School, an evening English-language school to teach Jewish immigrants English and life skills in their new home. It was the first such evening school in the country. "The Russian business so absorbs my thoughts that I have gone back to my early childhood longing to be a man," she wrote to her sister: "I am sure that if I were to be, I could mature plans of great benefit to them."

In 1893, she took a job at the Jewish Publication Society (JPS). Founded just five years earlier in Philadelphia by the famous Reform scholar Rabbi Joseph Krauskopf, JPS aimed to create a new body of Jewish American literature, written in English and with the needs of American Jews in mind. Szold labored for years to shape JPS into a publishing juggernaut.

Officially a secretary, in reality Henrietta worked for JPS as a senior editor and executive director. She oversaw the translation of the Hebrew Bible, Jewish books on philosophy and fiction, and ran the press' enormous Jewish Encyclopedia series. She edited the *American Jewish Year Book*, which, under her care, became one of the most important forums for discussing Jewish issues in the United States. Under Henrietta's editorship, the journal was home to debates in its pages concerning pogroms in Russia, Zionism, the massive influx of Jews into the United States, and the trial of Alfred Dreyfus in France. Most time-consuming of all, Henrietta translated into English all four volumes of the quasi-historical work *Legends of the Jews* by Louis Ginzberg, a Reform Rabbi and noted author.

Throughout all her many projects, Henrietta was never allowed to write her own name on works that she edited or translated: the most recognition she ever received was the appearance of the initials "H.S." at the end of an editor's note.

In 1902, while she was immersed in her work at JPS, Henrietta's father died, and she and her mother moved to New York City. There, Henrietta became friends with many Jewish scholars who took classes at the Jewish Theological Seminary (JTS), founded in 1886, and the home of the American Conservative Jewish movement. Henrietta longed to take classes at the seminary herself. She was eventually given permission by Solomon Schechter, JTS's president, to study, but only after he insisted that Henrietta formally, and humiliatingly, declare she had no interest in seeking ordination herself. She later worked as an editor and assistant at JTS - for a salary that was so small that the Chancellor himself acknowledged that he took advantage of the fact that Henrietta was far too well-bred a woman to ever try to negotiate for more.

When she was well into her 40s, Henrietta developed a romantic passion for Louis Ginzberg, who was 13 years her junior and a teacher at JTS. Some of Henrietta's friends warned that he seemed to be encouraging her feelings only so that she would continue to help his work. In fact, Ginzberg gave her scant recognition and no extra payment for the translations she performed of his books and other papers. In 1909, after years of close friendship with Henrietta, Ginzberg suddenly married a much younger woman, 23 year old Adele Katzenstein. (Ginzberg was 32 at the time.) The news of his sudden marriage devastated Henrietta.

Overwhelmed with sadness, Henrietta realized she needed a change of scene. She convinced her mother to go on a long trip with her to Europe and to the Land of Israel, which was then part of the Ottoman Empire.

Henrietta had been interested in the early Zionist movement ever since her work with Russian Jewish immigrants in Baltimore in the 1880s. Many of the Jews she taught were ardent Zionists, and in time both Henrietta and her mother Sophie became involved with Zionist causes in Baltimore and New York. Two years before, in 1907, Hadassah had been invited to lead a women's Zionist group in New York. Ever the ambitious intellectual, Henrietta had quickly transformed the club into a serious study group. Now she was finally going to see the Land of Israel, and the institutions that were being built by the early Jewish pioneers, with her own eyes.

She and her mother toured widely, visiting the impoverished cities of Jerusalem and Tiberias, where Jews lived in squalid conditions, and the new Jewish settlements of Zichron Yaakov and Tel Aviv. Henrietta wrote to her friend, the Jewish communal leader and Philadelphia Judge Mayer Sulzberger from her trip, describing both the beauty of the land and the vast task that was yet undone in building a Jewish state. She was particularly disturbed by the diseases that afflicted the many impoverished Jews and non-Jews she came across. "(M)y mother wept in Tiberias, she wept in Haifa, she wept in Jaffa, and she wept in Jerusalem. She wept because she saw so many eyes that had no function left but weeping, for they were blind from trachoma, and they belonged to owners whose lives were only worth weeping for. But even she learned to do more than weep on account of the physical misery everywhere..." Henrietta wrote.

Henrietta returned home a changed woman, shocked by the poverty she'd encountered and charged with the fervent belief that American Jews could help. She worked for a few years trying to find a practical way to help. Henrietta became the secretary of the new Federation of American Zionists, but was dismayed by its terrible financial state: running it was like "cleaning up other people's augean stables," she complained.

Finally, in 1912, Henrietta appealed to the Zionist women's study groups that were the source of so much of her own intellectual stimulation and companionship. On Purim that year, she convened a group of 38 women to create "a large organization of women Zionists" in New York. She envisioned her group becoming a national organization that would be named "Daughters of Zion." The New York chapter took the name Hadassah, the name of a popular Zionist study group there. Henrietta decided to focus on helping bring health care to the Jews in Israel. Nathan Straus, the Jewish philanthropist who owned Macy's department store, agreed to donate money to partially fund a visiting nursing system in Jerusalem: he challenged Henrietta to raise the rest of the money. This was Hadassa's first task: to raise $2,500 to build a nursing program.

The women of Hadassah rose to the challenge and raised the funds. In 1914, they sent two nurses to Jerusalem, Rose Kaplan and Rachel Landy. The nurses rented a small office in a house in Jerusalem and treated 5,000 patients in 1914 alone.

With the outbreak of World War I, the health needs in the Land of Israel increased. Henrietta and the Hadassah organization teamed up with other American Zionist groups to build a larger clinic in Jerusalem. They had to wait until the war ended to send supplies, and in 1918 Hadassah and other groups were able to send 45 medical staff, including American-trained doctors and nurses, as well as 400 tons of medical supplies. When she heard reports that the medical staff was having difficulty opening their clinic in the chaotic aftermath of the war, Henrietta set sail once again for Jerusalem. It was a journey that would transform the rest of her life. Henrietta was 59 years old when she arrived in Jerusalem. With the exception of family visits home, she never left.

Under Henrietta's leadership, the clinic she'd helped fund finally opened in Jerusalem under the name Hadassah Medical Organization. It prioritized women and children, and treated all patients regardless of ethnicity or religion. Soon, Hadassah's nascent hospital was helping local families receive subsidized food and milk for children and training nurses and other medical professionals. An increasingly organized group of women in the United States fundraised ever larger amounts to support the organization's medical work. Hadassah established other medical centers in other towns. In 1939, the Rothschild-Hadassah University Hospital opened in Jerusalem, the first teaching hospital in Mandatory Palestine.

With the rise of the Nazi party in Germany in 1933, Henrietta took on one final mammoth project, running the Jerusalem office of Youth Aliyah, bringing Jewish youths from Europe into the Land of Israel. Youth Aliyah was founded in Germany by Rebbetzin Recha Freir, an Orthodox Jewish teacher in Berlin, who desperately worked to obtain visas and transportation to help Jewish children leave Europe and start new lives in the land of Israel. Soon after 1933, she wrote to Henrietta for help with settling the children in Israel. The two women had a very difficult working relationship, but managed to cooperate enough to rescue between 7,000 and 11,000 Jewish children before the outbreak of World War II in 1939.

Henrietta raised funds for the effort and traveled around the land of Israel, asking kibbutzim to find room to house refugee children and lobbying British officials for support. She reveled in meeting with the children she helped, visiting them whenever she could. Henrietta never had biological children, but the thousands of children she aided through Youth Aliyah became like children to her.

One refugee child, whom Henrietta placed in Kibbutz Hulda in central Israel, terribly missed his parents in Germany, and wrote to Henrietta in a letter that captures just how much she meant to many of the children she helped. "Shmuel, our counselor, told us that you are the mother of all the children… I wanted to ask you, if you are everyone's mother, could you be my mother too… And I would play with you, and you would take walks with me on Shabbat, just the two of us, and you would tell me about flowers and dreams and other things," the boy wrote.

Late in her life, Henrietta finally did indulge in these beautiful activities with Jewish children in the fledgling state she'd done so much to help build. In 1951, six years after her death, the Israeli children's newspaper *Ha'aretz Shelanu* announced a plan to establish a Mother's Day in Israel, and asked its readers to suggest a date for the holiday. An eleven year old reader, Nehama Frankel, suggested Henrietta Szold's birthdate, in honor of her work rescuing Jewish children in the Youth Aliyah. Her birthday became Israel's Mother's Day.

The name was changed to Family Day in the year 2000, but the date remains the same: the 30th of Shevat, Henrietta's birthday, and a day of lasting tribute to this remarkable woman.

Sarah Schenirer
1883 - 1935

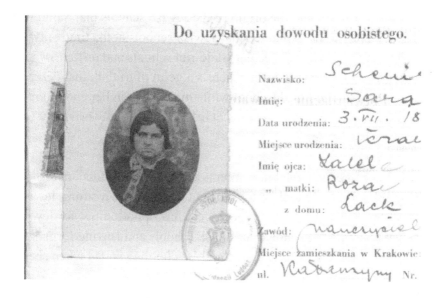

When Sarah Schenirer was born in 1883 in Krakow, the Jewish world around her was shifting. Her parents, Rabbi Bezalel Hakohen Scheinerer and Sheina Feigel Schenirer, were intensely Orthodox Jews who followed the Belzer Chassidic tradition. Yet among her eight siblings, religious life varied: several were less religious than their parents and one brother became completely secular. Sarah's friends displayed similarly modern tendencies: she recorded in her diary how shocked she was one Shabbat when a visiting friend turned on an electric light in Sarah's home.

Sarah was drawn to religion and knew that some people mocked her for that. "By the time I was six years old I had a nickname in school, 'Little Miss Hasid'," she wrote in her diary. While her sisters and friends gossiped and danced, Sarah would often remain on the sidelines, reading a Jewish work. "Even then it pained me to see my sisters acting in a barely Jewish way, without the slightest interest in a Jewish book," she later recalled. "Sometimes I would reproach a Jewish girl, and she would just laugh and respond that I was a Little Miss Hasid. But that didn't bother me, and I would just go back to being the way I was."

There are many legends about the origin of the Jewish schools that Sarah would go on to found: it's commonly explained that Jewish schools at the time only educated boys, so girls were left to attend secular, state-run schools and drifted away from Jewish observance as a consequence. There's a germ of truth in that description: Sarah attended a state-run Polish school while many boys in her community went to *cheders*, or Jewish elementary schools. Girls were generally privately educated in Jewish subjects at home.

In the 1920s, several educational movements arose to correct this imbalance, and some Jewish schools and school systems began to offer girls a strong Jewish education too. In Krakow, however, there were few opportunities for Jewish girls. Many followed Sarah's path, attending Polish schools and leaving formal education entirely at a very young age. Sarah's schooling ended when she was just 13 years old and became a dressmaker.

For years, she toiled sewing clothes, observing the Jewish women and girls who were customers, and mourning the way so many of them never seemed to mention anything connected with spirituality or Jewish ideas. "Customers were pleased with my work. Many of them would say to me that I put my heart and soul into it. I thought about that a lot," she wrote. "When I saw how concerned people were with the smallest detail when I was cutting and measuring their dresses, I would think to myself, 'And what do the 'garments' of their souls look like?'"

Sarah couldn't muster the same excitement for the clothes she stitched. She was intensely modest and eschewed many ordinary physical comforts. All her life, she resisted having her photograph taken; the only image that exists of her - an unflattering portrait in which she appears grumpy and put out - was taken because she needed a photo to obtain an official ID card in 1929.

In the evenings, after work, Sarah read voraciously. She devoured Jewish books and read many of Judaism's most foundational texts, more than making up for her lack of formal education. She also attended lectures at a local Christian women's club and loved to attend the Polish theater with her sister Matylda. Sensitive and often unworldly, Sarah dreamed of a way to share her love of higher learning.

She longed to meet a similarly spiritual man: she was very close with her younger brother Shimon, a very religious Belzer Chasid, and hoped that she might marry someone who was like him. Instead, her parents pressured her to marry a local businessman named Shmuel Nussbaum. He and Sarah courted for a year, and were never compatible. Yet Sarah gave in to her parents' pressure and reluctantly married him in 1910. Their marriage was unhappy from the start, and Sarah declared her intention to leave him; they finalized their divorce in 1913. They had no children.

The following year, World War I broke out, altering the life course of millions of people, Sarah included. Sarah and her family became refugees, and fled with many other Jews to Vienna. She began attending the Stumpergasse synagogue, and one Shabbat during Hanukkah in 1914, her ambition to teach and inspire other Jewish women and girls finally crystalized.

She was sitting in services when Rabbi Moshe David Flesch began to speak. "In his sermon, he depicted the greatness and sublimity of the historical figure of Judith, and through her, he eloquently and passionately called upon Jewish women and their daughters to act according to the model of this Jewish heroine," Sarah later described. She sat, riveted and intensely moved, then had a flash of despair that so many of the Jewish women she knew would never go to synagogue, would never have the chance to hear such stirring words.

"It struck me that our major problem is that our sisters know so little about our history, which alienates them from our people and its traditions," Sarah wrote. In that moment, she resolved to start a school for Jewish girls and share her excitement for their shared Jewish heritage.

Her father advised Sarah to consult with the Belzer Rebbe before getting started, so Sarah and her brother Shimon set out at once to visit Rabbi Yissachar Dov Rokeach, the third Belzer Rebbe. After hearing of Sarah's plan to open a school for Jewish girls, the Rebbe offered her two powerful words: *Beracha v'Hatzlacha*: Blessings and Success.

It wasn't easy to arrange, but by 1917 Sarah was finally able to return to Krakow and open a school. She had an initial student body of 25, most of them daughters of her dressmaking clients. Sitting in her classroom for the first time, Sarah recalled thinking that after sewing clothes for her pupils' mothers, "now I ask their mothers, will you also allow me to provide them with spiritual clothing?"

Sarah was an impassioned and popular teacher. She emphasized that each and every Jew has a personal relationship with the Divine: instead of going through the motions of Jewish observance, Sarah gave her students the tools to understand how Jewish traditions and rituals affected them personally. One towering Jewish educator, Rebbetzin Judith Grunfeld, who first started teaching under Sarah's guidance, recalled meeting Sarah for the first time at a retreat that Sarah organized in the Polish countryside. Girls gathered from all over Europe to learn, and Sarah lavished loving, individualized attention on every student: "it makes me realize that they are not just an anonymous crowd of girls," Rebbetzin Grunfeld later wrote; "Each one is an individual with a past and…a future. Each one is, in fact, a whole world."

Another compelling aspect of Sarah's teaching was emphasizing the way Jewish women have shaped Jewish history: students learned about brave, pious Jewish women who came before them. In fact, the name that Sarah chose for her school, *Bais Yaakov* - House of Jacob - also conveyed a powerful lesson about the centrality of Jewish women in Jewish history and tradition.

The number of students in Sarah's very first class, 25, had profound mystical connotations for Sarah. The number 25 has the same gematria value (total numerical value of the Hebrew letters) of the word *ko* ("thus") at the beginning of a key line in the Torah: when Moses stood atop Mount Sinai, God Spoke to him, telling Moses *Ko tomar l'beit Yaakov*: "Thus shall you say to the House of Jacob" (Exodus 19:3).

Jewish tradition explains the curious choice of the term "House of Jacob" - pronounced *Bais Yaakov* in Ashkenazi accented Hebrew - to mean that it refers specifically to the Jewish women. (Jacob was also known by the name Israel in the Torah, and in traditional Jewish commentaries, "The House of Israel" is seen to refer to Jewish men.) Thus, Moses was meant to relate the teachings of the Torah not only to the Jewish men, but to Jewish women as well. Sitting in her spartan classroom in Krakow one morning in 1917, Sarah Schenirer was becoming a link in that timeless chain, transmitting the lessons of Sinai to a new generation.

At the same time, Sarah set up other institutions. She held afternoon classes for older girls to attend once they finished state-run schools, though she never met with the same success among these older students, tired after attending a full day of school already. She help set up a teacher training course, offering up her own apartment to serve as the classroom, and a youth group called *Bnos* ("Daughters" in Hebrew). She started the *Bais Yaakov Journal*, which ran for sixteen years and became one of the most widely read Yiddish publications in the world.

Yet it was the *Beis Yaakov* school model that flourished most. The teachers Sarah trained began to help open new schools; within six years there were eight Bais Yaakov schools in Poland. In 1923, the newly formed Agudath Israel organization formally allied itself with the burgeoning movement, taking over much of the leadership and organizational functions. Sarah lost control of the movements she'd founded, but her influence continued to grow. Students began to refer to her as "Mama Sarah" and eagerly read her articles and attended the many lectures she continued to give.

In 1927, construction began on a large new *Beis Yaakov* building in Krakow. A plethora of Jewish dignitaries attended the groundbreaking, sitting on a raised dais separate from the crowd. One attendee observed that Sarah didn't stand with the other notables. Instead, modest as she always was, she gathered in the crowd with her beloved students. "Frau Schenirer, who stood with her disciples among the audience - shunning, as a pious woman of her type would do, glaring platform publicity - sent a prayer to God," the guest noted.

Sarah continued teaching, living in a dormitory with her students and spending her days immersed in intellectual and religious rigor. She became ill with cancer, eventually giving up the running of her beloved Krakow *Bais Yaakov*, in 1933. Yet she did find great happiness at last in her final years: in about the year 1930, she married Rabbi Yitzhak Landau, the very model of an elevated, spiritual Jewish man Sarah had always hoped to find.

Sarah passed away in 1935, one of the most beloved women in the Jewish world. She was spared seeing the murder of her five living siblings, of her students, and of virtually everyone she knew and admired, from Rabbi Moshe David Flesch who'd so inspired her in Vienna, to her friends and neighbors, in the concentration camps of Nazi Europe.

By 1937, two years after Sarah Schenirer's death, there were 248 Bais Yaakov schools educating 35,000 girls. Today, Bais Yaakov schools continue to thrive the world over. In Israel alone, there are over 100 Bais Yaakov schools, educating over 15,000 girls. Virtually every city in the world with a sizable Jewish population is home to at least one Bais Yaakov school: the thousands of students who attend them consider themselves Sarah's spiritual descendents.

Selma Mair
1884 - 1984

When Selma Mair was just five years old, tragedy struck: she was one of five children in a poor Orthodox Jewish family in Hanover, Germany when her beloved mother died in childbirth. This harrowing loss led Selma to want to help others and learn all she could about medicine. She enrolled in nursing school, an audacious and unusual move for a young Jewish woman at that time, and worked in the Salomon Heine Hospital in Hamburg, gaining intense practical experience.

In 1913, Germany allowed Jewish women to sit for nurses diploma exams for the very first time. Selma and another Jewish woman took the exam and became the first Jewish nurses licensed in Germany. "We both passed the examinations with 'very good'," Selma later recalled, "and the German doctors especially praised our theoretical knowledge."

Finally fully licensed, Selma had her pick of jobs in Germany. Instead, a visit from the great German Jewish doctor Dr. Moshe Wallach changed her life. An ardent Zionist, Dr. Wallach had founded Shaare Tzedek Hospital, an Orthodox Jewish hospital just outside the Old City in Jerusalem, in 1902. Now, he was returning to Germany to find a professional who could assist him in bringing modern medicine to the Middle East. Selma and Dr. Wallach had much in common: they were both Orthodox Jews and ardent Zionists. They each were determined to uphold the highest standard of medicine. Selma accepted his offer to become Shaarei Tzedek's head nurse and matron.

It was a difficult move. At the time, Jerusalem had neither electricity nor piped water. The city was unimaginably primitive compared with Hamburg. Even getting to the Middle East seemed a nearly impossible challenge in the midst of World War I. The mores of the time also dictated that a young woman like Selma could not possibly travel alone.

"It was not so easy to travel from Germany to Palestine in those days," Selma later recorded. "First I had to have an exit permit from the military authorities in Germany, as well as an entry permit for Palestine. And thus it continued. I traveled from Berlin to Budapest. There I got on the Balkan train to Constantinople. There I met Arthur Ruppin, who, as a Zionist, had to flee, and with him some other prominent personalities who had engaged in Zionist activities. From Constantinople the journey continued over the Taurus and Amanus mountain ranges by car which was as wide as the whole mountain pass and which took us to the Hadjaz train, in Damascus. There we had to stay over for a few days until there was a train to Jerusalem. The whole trip lasted four weeks." Arthur Ruppin would go on to become one of the founders of Tel Aviv. Selma Mair was about to transform medicine in the nascent Jewish community in Palestine. It was a heady time to be young and idealistic, building the new Jewish state.

In Jerusalem, she was shocked by the poor conditions she faced. People traveled by donkey and camel, and there was very little food in the city. On one terrifying occasion, Turkish troops fighting the British bombarded the hospital. Even more deadly, typhus raged throughout Jerusalem, and Selma's first months in Shaarei Tzedek were consumed with treating the hundreds of gravely ill patients who lined up each day to be seen in the hospital. Patient and kind, Selma soon became known as "Shvester Selma," or Sister Selma, to the many people who flocked to be under her care.

Selma was adamant about imposing the high standards she learned in Germany on Shaare Tzedek's nursing staff. Battling hunger, dirt, superstition and a lack of supplies, Selma gradually transformed Shaare Tzedek into a modern, efficient Jewish hospital. She trained generations of nurses and midwives. She also acted as the hospital's director as it grew, oversaw the building and equipment, and made sure that the hospital's kitchens adhered to the highest kosher standards. When Dr. Wallach operated, it was Selma Mair who assisted him. Patients travelled to see her from across the city. On days when "Shvester Selma" had office hours, the line of patients waiting for her consultations sometimes stretched around the block. Selma oversaw the care of scores of Jews who were injured during the Arab pogroms against the Jews of Hebron in 1929, and coordinated care for polio victims during periodic epidemics in Jerusalem.

In 1936, Selma helped found Shaare Tzedek's nursing school, teaching all of the school's practical nursing classes. One of the express aims of the school was to provide a place for Jewish women to flee Nazi Germany and learn a trade in the Land of Israel. By giving them a place to study and live, Selma Mair and Shaarei Tzedek saved the lives of a generation of young Jewish nurses.

In the midst of her incredibly busy career, Selma also made time to become a mother. Though she never married, Selma Mair was a mother to three girls through adoption. Zamura was an ill child whose parents abandoned her; Selma became her loving mother. Simcha was left abandoned after her mother died and her father was drafted into the Ottoman army, until Selma adopted her. The third child Selma adopted was a girl named Bolissa whose family had come to Palestine from Syria, riding on a camel. Bolissa's mother died and she herself was very ill. When Bolissa's father abandoned her at Shaare Tzedek, Selma adopted her, arranging her education and later for her to stay with a foster family in Germany. During the Holocaust, Bolissa's foster family was murdered but she was able to return to Palestine, thanks to her Syrian passport. Selma enrolled Bolissa in nursing school in Jerusalem. During Israel's War of Independence in 1948, Bolissa was killed by a British bomb on Ben Yehuda Street in the middle of the city.

Writing about her life in 1973, Selma Mair noted that "because I lost my mother very early and therefore had a rather difficult youth, a strong need grew in me to give people that which I had missed so much: mother-love and love of human beings. Therefore I chose the profession of nursing." Her motto, she explained, was a quote by the modern Bengali poet Rabindranath Tagore, which resonated with her deeply: "I slept and dreamt that life was joy. I awoke and saw that life was duty. I acted and behold duty was joy."

True to her commitment to serve others, Selma kept working at Shaare Tzedek for sixty eight years, until her death at age 100.

Sarah Aaronsohn
1890 - 1917

Tall, stylish, beautiful, and gregarious, Sarah Aaronsohn was the embodiment of a new type of Jewish woman: a vivid member of the "*chalutzim*", the pioneer generation which built modern day Israel in the early 1900s, when it was still under Ottoman Turkish rule.

Her parents Ephraim and Malka Aaronsohn moved from Romania to the Land of Israel in 1882, driven both by anti-Semitic pogroms that were roiling Romania and also by their idealistic Zionist belief in building a new Jewish homeland. They settled in the town of Zichron Yaakov in Israel's north, where they helped build the nascent Jewish community. By the time Sarah was born there in 1890, the Aaronsohns were prominent in the area. Sarah had five siblings, including an older brother Aaron, who became one of the world's foremost agronomists, an expert in soil management and crop production.

Sarah inherited her parents' pride and idealism. Her mother's family was descended from prominent rabbis and could trace their lineage directly to King David, and Sarah apparently saw herself as a natural and fearless leader. As a child, she begged her father for a horse. He eventually gave in, and Sarah spent her teenage years riding across the landscape of northern Israel, becoming an accomplished horsewoman and a crack shot with a pistol. Like her brothers, Sarah was a gifted linguist, and easily learned Hebrew, Yiddish, English, French, German, Turkish and Arabic, including the various dialects of Arabic spoken in the region.

She visited Central Europe with her family, and became Zichron Yaakov's best seamstress, copying the European fashions she'd observed there and which filled the fashion magazines she subscribed to. Although the local girls' school ended in middle school, Sarah continued her education, studying agronomics along with her famous brother Aaron. By the time she was fifteen, she worked as Aaron's secretary. When he was away (most notably, helping the Turkish authorities thwart devastating locust infestations and gaining adulation and fame along the way), Sarah took his place as the representative of Zichron Yaakov's farming interests in their relations with the local Ottoman Turkish authorities.

In 1914, Sarah married Chaim Abraham, an older Jewish immigrant from Bulgaria, and moved with him to Istanbul, where he had business interests. Many of her friends believed at the time that she was only marrying Chaim because of an old-fashioned but entrenched custom of the time: it was unthinkable for a younger daughter to get married before her older sister. By marrying Chaim, Sarah made it possible for her younger sister Rivka to get married to the love of her life (and, some said, the love of Sarah's life as well), a dashing young Jewish botanist from Zichron Yaakov named Absalom Feinberg.

Sadly, Sarah's marriage was not a happy one, and the following year, as Turkey was in the midst of fighting World War I alongside Germany, Sarah left her husband and travelled home by train to Zichron Yaakov.

The sights that Sarah saw from her train carriage as it moved through the Ottoman countryside horrified her. Ottoman Turks were in the midst of conducting what would be known as the Armenian Genocide, which saw the murder of one million men, women and children during World War I. Sarah later described seeing hundreds of bodies being loaded onto trains, and witnessing the brutal murder of up to 5,000 Armenians, whose bodies were then piled in a pyramid with kindling, and set on fire. "In front of her very eyes, she saw the Armenians being tortured by the Turks," Sarah's brother Aaron wrote in his diary; "She saw hundreds of dead Armenians, lying on the ground, unburied, devoured by wild dogs."

The Ottoman Turks who administered the Land of Israel made no secret of their hatred of Jews, and Sarah feared that the genocide she witnessed against the Armenians of the Ottoman Empire would next be directed against Jews if the Ottomans won the war. (In 1914, at the onset of the war, Sultan Mehmed V announced a *jihad*, a religious war against non-Muslims within its territory and without.)

When she returned to Zichron Yaakov, Sarah was determined to do all she could to aid Great Britain, which was fighting Ottoman forces across the Middle East. Along with her older brothers Aaron and Alexander, her sister Rivka, brother-in-law Absalom Feinberg, and about forty other local Jewish youth, Sarah helped form a secret group dedicated to helping Britain win the war. These idealistic young Jews named their organization NILI, an acronym for the Biblical phrase *Netzach Yisrael Lo Yeshaker*, "the Eternal One of Israel does not lie down" nor relent, but rather vanquishes the enemies of Israel (Samuel I 15:29).

NILI spies wanted to help Britain invade the Land of Israel from their bases in Egypt, but at first British forces rebuffed the group's top-secret overtures. Finally, in late 1916, Aaron Aaronsohn managed to cross Turkish lines and traversed the Sinai Peninsula to reach Cairo and convince British forces there to trust the Jewish spy ring.

Sarah took over the running of NILI. (Historian Scott Anderson has written that her capable and strong-willed leadership was likely enhanced by the fact that several members of the group seem to have been in love with her.) Together, the spies of NILI gathered intelligence on Turkish troop movements, fortifications, railroads, water locations, troop movements, and weather patterns. Sarah encoded messages and communicated with British headquarters by sending secret codes every two weeks to the British warship *Managam* anchored off the coast of Palestine, using light signals to convey information to the ship.

NILI also received funds from supporters in America and helped distribute money to the Jews in Ottoman-controlled Israel who were near starvation due to Turkish anti-Semitic policies and ruinous taxes on the Jewish community. Though they suspected that a Jewish spy ring was operating somewhere in the land of Israel, Ottoman forces had no idea that Sarah was leading the Middle East's largest group of secret operatives, which was observing their every move.

In July, 1917, Sarah wrote a letter to her sister Rivka, who was visiting the United States, raising money for Jewish settlement. It was one of the last letters she ever wrote. "I have a large role in the work here, and if we have to endanger ourselves, my dear one, I think not of it," Sarah wrote. "The work is dear and holy to me….we were promised the land of Israel...and we have merited to see it."

In Autumn 1917, British troops stopped sending the frigate to pick up NILI's messages, and Sarah turned to homing pigeons, a method of communication she'd previously distrusted but now felt she had no choice but to use. She sent pigeons to British authorities, trying desperately to convey to Britain's General Allenby valuable information that would enable him to traverse the Negev Desert and attack Turkish troops in Beersheva.

In September, 1917, disaster struck. One of NILI's homing pigeons landed on a house belonging to the Turkish governor of Caesarea. Ottoman officials found the message the bird carried and decoded it, realizing that a large pro-British spying ring was operating with impunity somewhere in northern Israel. They made finding the spy ring's members and leaders their priority.

One by one, Ottoman forces rounded up members of NILI's spy ring, using torture to extract information. Finally, on October 1, 1917, Sarah Aaronsohn was arrested and taken to a makeshift Turkish prison in Zichron Yaakov. For several days, she was made to watch her mother and father being brutally whipped until they were severely injured. Then, Turkish officials took Sarah to her family home, tied her to a gatepost, and beat her brutally with long truncheons. Drawing on near-superhuman reserves of strength, Sarah refused to divulge information about NILI. Instead, she taunted her captors before losing consciousness, assuring them they would lose the war and be punished for their oppression of Jews and their massacre of Armenians.

After nearly of week of agony, Sarah was informed that she would be transferred to prison in Damascus where she would face even greater torture. She asked if she could be allowed to enter her family home one last time to bathe and change her clothes. Early one morning, as most of Zichron Yaakov slept, Sarah was led down the town's main street to her family home, which stood abandoned, its inhabitants imprisoned. As Sarah walked, she sang a Yiddish song about a little bird that flies away. This was no innocent tune: it was her final signal to her surviving NILI comrades that the ring was broken and they were to cease any further activity in order to save themselves.

Once in the house, Sarah opened a secret compartment in a wall and retrieved a hidden handgun. Concealing the gun in the folds of her dress, she entered the bathroom and turned on the water. She scribbled a hasty note, tossed it out of the window, and then shot herself in the mouth. Instead of dying instantly, she lingered for three excruciating days before passing away on October 10, 1917. She was twenty seven years old.

Just three weeks after her untimely death, Britain issued the landmark Balfour Declaration, throwing its support behind the establishment of a Jewish state in the Land of Israel. Less than a year later, on September 25, 1918, Turkish troops finally surrendered to Britain near Megiddo, in Israel's north, ending 400 years of Ottoman rule over the area.

Today, Sarah Aaronsohn's house still stands and is a museum dedicated to the astonishing accomplishments of her NILI spy ring. It houses an official letter from British Captain Baron William Ormsby-Gore acknowledging that Britain could not have won World War I without the material aid of the NILI spies. There is also the last letter that Sarah Aaronsohn wrote, moments before she shot herself.

In it, she asks us all to "describe all our suffering to those who shall come after we have passed away, and tell them about our martyrdom, and let them know that Sarah has asked that each drop of blood be avenged...."

Golda Meir
1898 - 1978

One of Golda Meir's earliest memories was hiding with her family in their apartment building in Kiev while an armed mob rampaged through the streets looking for Jews to attack. "I can remember how I stood on the stairs that led to the second floor, where another Jewish family lived, holding hands with their little daughter and watching our fathers trying to barricade the entrance with boards of wood...I remember how scared I was and how angry that all my father could do to protect me was to nail a few planks together while we waited for the hooligans to come," she later recalled.

Those eloquent words were written by Golda in English, not in Yiddish, which was her first language, nor in Hebrew, the language of the country she would eventually lead when she served as Israel's Prime Minister 1969-1974. A few years after that terrifying ordeal, Golda's family moved to America, like so many eastern European Jews. They settled in Milwaukee.

Golda remembered her years in Milwaukee as a time of transformation. The scars of pogroms in Ukraine still haunted her family: when they went to attend their first Labor Day parade in their new home, Golda's little sister, Zipke, saw police officers on horses and became hysterical, screaming "It's the Cossacks! It's the Cossacks!" For Golda, the sight of police officers protecting Jews and other citizens instead of harming them was a profound lesson in how free people could live.

Golda's family was filled with strong personalities, and their home was often consumed with arguments. Golda's mother wanted her to leave school at fourteen and work, while Golda wished to go on to high school; instead, Golda ran away to live with her older sister Shayna and Shayna's husband Shammai in Denver. There, Golda recalled, life really opened up for me." She attended high school in Denver, but her real education occurred in the evenings in her sister's home.

Shayna and Shammai were part of a radical Zionist social group in Denver, and each evening after dinner a teenaged Golda would listen to the impassioned political debates. Years later she recalled "it was to the Socialist Zionists that I found myself listening most attentively…I understood and responded fully to the idea of a national home for the Jews - one place on the face of the earth where Jews could be free and independent - and I took it for granted that in such a place no one would be in want or be exploited or live in fear of other men."

That early Zionist idealism was to guide Golda throughout her life. It was at those fiery evenings at Shayna's home that Golda first met Morris Myerson, a brilliant, self-educated Zionist thinker whom she later married. They shaped her intellectually, too, giving her a passionately political view of the world and the possibility of political change.

Golda eventually returned to Milwaukee, finished high school and college, and became a teacher. Her real passion, however, was advocating for the establishment of a Jewish state. In Golda's absence, her father had become an active pillar of Milwaukee's Jewish life, and, for a time, Golda joined him, raising money to aid Jews during World War I and advocating for immigration to the Land of Israel and building a Jewish country there.

She wouldn't take no for an answer. During the High Holidays, for instance, Golda recalled, "I put up a box just outside the synagogue, and people walking out on their way home had no alternative other than to hear at least part of what I had to say about the Labor Zionist platform."

In 1921, Golda and Morris Myerson - now her husband - traveled to Mandatory Palestine with Golda's sister, Shayna, and her children. Golda and Morris moved to Kibbutz Merhavia, in Israel's north, and Golda reveled in the hard work and privations of the kibbutz. Ever the charismatic leader, Golda seemed to rise to the top of every organization she joined. She soon was elected to the kibbutz steering committee, and given special permission to address delegates at a convention in Yiddish instead of Hebrew, which she was still learning.

Morris wasn't cut out for kibbutz life, and Golda and he experimented with living first in Tel Aviv, and then in Jerusalem, where their two children were born. Their marriage was an unhappy one, and it unraveled completely in 1928 when an acquaintance offered Golda a job as secretary of Moetzet Hapoalot, the women's labor council of the huge Histadrut labor union. The job involved extensive travel abroad and long hours, and Golda withdrew from her family life.

She later recalled: "What I do regret - and bitterly so - is that although Morris and I remained married to each other and loving each other until the day he died in my house in 1951 (when symbolically enough, I was away), I was not able to make a success of our marriage after all. The decision I took in 1928 actually marked the start of our separation, although it didn't become final for almost ten years."

Golda rose in Histadrut, eventually heading its political department. In her memoirs, she relishes descriptions of the myriad technical details that bedeviled the *Yishuv*, the nascent Jewish state that was being built in the land of Israel. Throughout the 1930s, as Hitler persecuted Jews, refugees flocked into the land of Israel. That "meant that 60,000 men, women and children had to be absorbed at once by a population of fewer than 400,000 that was barely able to make ends meet in any case, and they all had somehow to survive not only growing Arab terror, but also the indifference - not to say hostility - of the (British) mandatory government."

With the outbreak of World War II, Golda became part of a top-secret program through the Va'ad Hapoel, the Zionist General Council, to raise 75,000 British pounds sterling to smuggle into embattled Jewish communities in Nazi-occupied countries, allowing them to buy food, arms, and to possibly smuggle Jews out to freedom. By the end of the war, Golda was head of the Jewish Agency's Jerusalem office, and an even greater task was beginning: fighting for a Jewish state, first diplomatically, and then in Israel's War of Independence. Twice, Golda traveled to Jordan for secret meetings with King Abdullah, who promised to refrain from joining any Arab attack on the *Yishuv*, which was about to declare a Jewish state. (It was a promise he would soon break.) Golda was also dispatched to America to lobby for the establishment of a Jewish country and to raise funds to help it in any forthcoming war of independence.

By May 14, 1948, Israel's Independence Day, Golda was back home in Israel. She took part in last minute discussions - including deciding on the name of the forthcoming country (she voted against "Rock of Israel") - and was present when Ben-Gurion declared, on behalf of the National Council, representing the Jewish people in the Land of Israel and the Zionist movement, the State of Israel.

"The State of Israel!" Golda wrote near the end of her life. "My eyes filled with tears, and my hands shook. We had done it. We had brought the Jewish state into existence - and I, Golda Mobovitch Meyerson, had lived to see the day. Whatever happened now, whatever price any of us would have to pay for it, we had re-created the Jewish national home….As Ben-Gurion read, I thought again about my children and the children they would have, how different their lives would be from mine and how different my own life would be from what it had been in the past…"

In the months that followed, Golda worked feverishly to support the struggling new nation. Within hours of Ben-Gurion's declaration, the armies of Jordan, Egypt, Lebanon, Syria and Iraq attacked Israel. Two days after Israel's establishment, Ben-Gurion dispatched Golda to the United States to raise desperately needed funds to purchase arms and other supplies. The trip was impromptu, and Golda left straight to the airport with only the dress she was wearing and her coat. Her goal in America was to raise $50 million; instead, criss-crossing the country and giving speech after speech, she managed to raise $150 million.

Everywhere she went, Golda seemed to inspire people, bringing out the best in others and kindling Jewish pride. She had a sharp sense of humor and was often self-deprecating, relying on Yiddish witticisms to cut through pomposity and speak home truths. Abba Eban said her "talent lay in the simplification of issues. She went straight to the crux and center of each problem…she tended to interrupt (interlocutors) with an abrupt request for the bottom line."

In 1948 Golda became Israel's ambassador to the Soviet Union: she was welcomed by Joseph Stalin, who was implacably opposed to the Jewish state and repressed Jewish life in the Soviet Union. With only a paltry diplomatic allowance from Israel, Golda organized the diplomatic mission in Moscow like a kibbutz, with communal eating and an egalitarian spirit.

On her first Rosh Hashanah in Moscow, Golda and her colleagues prepared to attend Moscow's Great Synagogue (one of only three synagogues allowed to operate in the entire city), and walked up to the building, expecting to see the approximately 2,000 Jews who usually attended services there. Filled with KGB informers, the synagogue was avoided by many Moscow Jews. Yet on the evening Golda attended services there, a crowd filled the street.

"(A) crowd of close to 50,000 people was waiting for us. For a minute I couldn't grasp what had happened – or even who they were. And then it dawned on me. They had come - those good, brave Jews - in order to be with us, to demonstrate their sense of kinship and to celebrate the establishment of the State of Israel. Within seconds they had surrounded me, almost lifting me bodily, almost crushing me, saying my name over and over again…"

Golda became Israel's Foreign Minister in 1965. Prime Minister Ben-Gurion insisted she choose a Hebrew-sounding last name for the appointment; that's when she shortened Meyerson to Meir, which means "illuminated" in Hebrew. In a tumultuous and intense career, one of her notable and lasting achievements was forging close relations between Israel and developing nations in Africa, East Asia and Latin America.

Israeli diplomat Yehuda Avner recalled a meeting with Golda and her diplomatic staff in those years. "In a tone full of conviction and in a Hebrew filled with Milwaukee-sounding pronunciations, she told us there were two things she wanted to drum into our heads. 'One is, coming to the aid of African States now winning independence after decades of colonial rule is an emotional thing for me…" To the staff's surprise, she picked up Theodor Herzl's novel *Altneuland* about the founding of a Jewish state, and read in a voice filled with emotion a passage describing how a Jewish state could one day aid newly independent nations in Africa.

"Golda Meir's matriarchal features wore an earnest and dedicated expression, and her voice went husky as she avowed, 'It has fallen to me to carry out Dr. Theodor Herzl's vision. Each year, more and more African States are gaining national independence. Like us, their freedom was won only after years of struggle. Like us, they had to fight for their statehood. And like us, nobody handed them their sovereignty on a silver platter. In a world divided between 'the haves' and the 'have-nots,' Israel's nation-building experience is uniquely placed to lend a helping hand… We have a vast amount of expertise to offer. For this purpose I have set up a new division for international cooperation - note what I say; international cooperation, not international aid - and you people are going to help staff it…" Avner recalled.

Golda was the world's only female foreign minister at the time, and she eschewed all titles and honorifics: she traveled economy class, and washed her laundry by hand in hotel sinks on business trips.

She left the Foreign Ministry in 1966 and soon led the new unified Labor Party in Israel. After Prime Minister Levi Eshkol died suddenly in 1969, Golda was asked to assume the position of Prime Minister. She acquiesced out of a sense of duty, and cried when Israel's Knesset unanimously voted on her candidacy. At 71, Golda had given her all to Israel. She'd recently been treated for lymphoma - a fact that she hid from the public, going for medical treatment at Hadassah Hospital in the middle of the night - and was enjoying life as a private citizen after her years as Foreign Minister. "I had planned to come to Palestine, to go to Merhavia, to be active in the labor movement," she recalled thinking at the moment she became Prime Minister. Instead of that quiet life she'd longed for, her years were filled with high pressure work and public service.

Golda's premiership was dominated and marked by the surprise attack that Egypt and Syria launched together in the early morning of October 6, 1973, and which led to the grinding, nineteen day long Yom Kippur War. Facing a massive troop buildup on their borders, Golda resisted calling up Israel's military reserves until the last moment, a decision she regretted for the rest of her life. Even though her Labor Party won a plurality in Israel's 1973 elections, Golda was unable to form a coalition, and resigned from office. Her successor, Yitzhak Rabin, was the first sabra - Israeli-born citizen - to lead the Jewish state.

In her retirement, Golda wrote a best-selling volume of memoirs. "Like my generation, this generation of sabras will strive, struggle, make mistakes and achieve," she concluded in her autobiography. "Like us, they are totally committed to the development and security of the State of Israel and to the dream of a just society here. Like us, they know that for the Jewish people to remain a people, it is essential that there be a Jewish state where Jews can live as Jews, not on sufferance and not as a minority. I am certain that they will bring at least as much credit to the Jewish people everywhere as we tried to bring."

Nehama Leibowitz
1905 - 1997

Nehama Leibowitz was a woman of great contradictions. Born into an upper class, educated, Orthodox family in Riga in 1905, she grew up surrounded by erudition and scholarship. Her older brother Prof. Yeshayahu Leibowitz became one of Israel's most notable academics and he remained her greatest confidante and friend throughout their lives. (Yeshayahu and Nehama each won the Israel Prize, Israel's highest academic honor, Nehama in 1956 and Yeshayahu in 1993). She was brilliant and known for having little patience for fools. Yet for much of her career, Nehama taught - and indeed glorified in teaching - working class people without the advantages of education that she herself had enjoyed.

Having grown up in luxury, she embraced a spartan lifestyle in Israel that was extreme even by the standards of her austere adopted homeland. By turns cutting and impatient, she was also capable of great kindness. (Friends recalled her giving away her possessions to the poor, including a new suit she'd just bought for herself, and her parents' heavy, monogrammed wedding silver, which she donated to Russian immigrants.) She could be funny and harsh, and inspired great loyalty in her many students. Her approach to Torah study revolutionized Jewish learning, changing the way Jews approach the texts of the Torah and its commentaries, and the questions that are asked when studying Torah to this day.

From an early age, Nehama seemed destined for great things. Her family moved to Berlin in 1910, and Nehama studied at many of Germany's most prestigious schools, gaining a Ph.D. from the University of Marburg in 1930; her thesis was about translating the Bible into German. She was an ardent Zionist, teaching in Jewish high schools while she worked on her Ph.D., using a method that was unheard of in Germany at the time, speaking Hebrew in class as if it were a living language. Steeped in German literature, she embraced the newly-spoken language of modern Hebrew, and yearned to help build a Jewish land.

In 1930, immediately after gaining her doctorate, Nehama and her husband Yedidyah Lipman Leibowitz moved to Israel. (Her marriage was yet another way in which Nehama was unusual in the extreme: Yedidyah was her uncle, her father's brother. The nature of their shocking marriage was the source of great speculation, with some people positing that it was platonic; they had no children.) After a brief trip back to Germany to persuade her parents to emigrate, Nehama returned to Israel and never again set foot outside the Jewish state. Even when her fame had spread far and wide and she received invitations from abroad, Nehama remained in Israel, lecturing all around the country, and making a great effort to include even the most obscure, poor and far-flung Israeli towns and settlements in her busy teaching schedule.

In 1941, Nehama began teaching in Jerusalem's *Beit Midrash l'Morot Mizrahi Yerushalayim*, a teacher training college for young women from a Mizrahi (Middle Eastern) background. Many of the girls were poor; some spoke only broken Hebrew. Nehama was a demanding teacher, and expected excellence from her young students. She started writing worksheets on the weekly Torah portion, asking her students to evaluate the differing views on the portion offered by some of the most central Torah commentators through the ages, such as Rashi (1040-1105), Ramban (1194-1270), Rashbam (1085-1158), ibn Ezra (1089-1167), and others.

Nehama was curious not only in hearing her students describe these commentators' views: she designed her worksheets for exploring contradictions between their approaches, and to reconcile differing views of the Torah's text. She coined a question that today is a central query heard in virtually every Jewish school the world over: What's bothering Rashi? In her worksheets, Nehama wasn't only interested in getting her students to understand Rashi's views and comments: she prompted her students to think critically, asking themselves why Rashi thought certain details in the Torah were worth mentioning and parsing in the first place.

Though difficult, the worksheets proved incredibly popular. Each Shabbat, groups of students would sit on a lawn near the school, discussing their answers. At the end of the year, the students had a request: during the Summer break, could they have more worksheets? Nehama agreed, and mailed worksheets to her students each week. Soon, requests began coming in from people who saw the sheets: could Nehama mail them worksheets, too? Each week, many of the worksheets she'd sent out were returned to her by mail: Nehama would laboriously go through them, commenting on their answers, and mail heavily annotated worksheets back.

Within a few years, Nehama was mailing out thousands of sheets every week, and corresponding with the recipients. She kept up this enormous project for 29 years, until the strain became too much. In 1971, Nehama announced the end of her weekly worksheets with a public letter to her legions of students: "Many thanks to all my students, near and far, in Israel and overseas, whose questions and replies, perseverance and love of Torah have been a source of strength, pleasure and deepened insight… In the full sense of the phrase, I have learned more from my students than from anyone else," she wrote.

"…There were regulars who wrote dutifully week by week, year in and year out…I wish here to pay tribute to those who contacted me under difficult conditions after a hard day's work, in the burning sun during a break in the field; to the streetsweeper who wrote in the height of a rainstorm after doing his day's stint, to the machinist dropping me a line during the lunch-break amidst the noise of the factory, to the nurse using her precious hours of rest after a back-breaking night shift… There were soldiers who wrote to me under conditions defying description: coastguards, World War II volunteers in the Libyan desert and Jewish Brigade, fighters in the War of Liberation delivering their notes to me personally from a forward position during a chance lull in the Capital's shelling when the postal service was at a standstill.…"

"I am enthralled by this vast army of old and young, mothers and girls, teachers male and female, clerks and laborers…hundreds of thousands (literally!) studying Torah for its own sake. For our joint studies involved no certificates, examinations, marks, prizes; no credits, scholarships, income-tax rebates but simply the joy so deep of the one who studies Torah."

Though her weekly correspondence was at an end, Nehama's appetite for bringing her distinctive questions to a wider audience was not. She wrote a series of books, titled simply "Studies" in each of the Five Books of Moses: Genesis, Exodus, Leviticus, Numbers, and Deuteronomy. These five volumes brought Nechama's work to a wider audience. Her set of books became a mainstay in Jewish homes and libraries around the world.

Nechama was a devotee of the dictum by Rambam (1138-1204): "Accept the truth from wherever it comes." In addition to the most famous Jewish sages, Nehama's books included quotes and comments by less mainstream scholars such as Yitzhak Heinemann (1875-1957), Simha Reuven Edelmann (1821-1892), Martin Buber (1878-1965), Haim Hazaz (1898-1973), and many others. Not all of these commentators were traditionally observant, but Nehama recognized the wisdom in their observations on the Torah's eternal truths. She did not overtly address contemporary political issues, but her tone throughout her books is warmly liberal and open-minded, shaping the way Jews approached the Torah's text in the modern era.

Her observations convey her great respect for ordinary people who choose to spend their time in the holy pursuit of studying Torah. "The Torah is not the property of a privileged caste of priests and initiates," she wrote in *Studies in Devarim* (Deuteronomy). "It is not in heaven but in our midst. It is the duty of all to study, teach and practice its tenets."

In her Studies, Nehama pointed out times when our Biblical patriarchs and matriarchs displayed human flaws and frailties. She displayed a commitment to Zionism and stressed Jews' eternal attachment to the Land of Israel. One message that comes through in all her Studies is the potential glory of every person. In writing about the patriarch Jacob, for instance, in *Studies on Bereshit* (Genesis),

Nehama declares that "Jacob's communion with his Creator, his beholding of the Divine Presence at Bethel did not turn him into a recluse, contemplating the Heavenly mysteries. Rather his experience spurred him to practical action, to promoting welfare and justice in society."

As in this ideal vision of Jewish activity, Nehama herself never stopped pushing herself to do more. In the 1980s, she began working on new classes for Israel's Open University (which was open to all citizens), ever devoted to democratizing knowledge and education. She continued to teach in schools across Israel and kept up a busy schedule of traveling and lecturing across Israel until shortly before her death at the age of 92 in 1997.

In time, Nehama became a national treasure. People recognized her on the street and would ask her questions about the Torah. In one widely shared and typical example, during the height of the Intifadah, Nehama was due to give a lecture in the town of Efrat, in the West Bank. Soldiers stopped Nehama's taxi and explained that due to unrest along the road, only vehicles escorted by military personnel were allowed to travel on it that day. The taxi driver was outraged. "Do you know who this is?" he asked an officer present; "This is Nehama Leibowitz!"

The officer was chastened: "Why didn't you say so?" he asked, and ordered a soldier to drive her to Efrat immediately, and also to take her home. As the soldier drove off, the officer yelled after him: "and you should go in and listen to the class! It won't do you any harm!"

Nehama left instructions that after her death, she was to have a simple funeral with no eulogies. On her tombstone, she is described as "Nehama Leibowitz: teacher." After her casket was lowered into the ground, her nephew said to the assembled mourners that, as Nehama had no children of her own, all those who felt like a son to Nehama - as he did - should join him in the Kaddish prayer, traditionally recited by a son for a parent. As her funeral concluded, from all across the cemetery, mourners joined in, reciting the Mourners Kaddish for Nehama Leibowitz, their beloved mentor and teacher.

Miriam Rothschild
1908 - 2005

When Miriam Rothschild was just twenty one, a prominent naturalist invited her to conduct research at a biological marine research station in Naples. If the job was offered to anyone else in her position - Miriam was an inexperienced aristocrat studying English literature at the University of London at the time - this invitation might have seemed precipitous. But Miriam wasn't any ordinary young undergraduate: throughout her long life, she charmed and changed virtually everyone she came across. Miriam accepted the research position and spent a carefree summer conducting valuable experiments on molluscs.

She was so charming that when a volcanic explosion resulted in the formation of a small new island in the Bay of Naples that summer, her colleagues rushed to name it Mont Miriam in her honor. It was a sign of admiration and friendship that marked her entire life. After her death in 2005, a British newspaper eulogized her "huge and unfailing enthusiasm for life's intricacies and elegance" and her "love, obsession and compassion for living things of all kinds." Miriam was a force of nature: a warm companion; a persuasive opponent when she needed to be; a brilliant scientist; a passionate advocate for Jewish and other causes; and a loyal friend.

Miriam's family lineage was impeccably aristocratic: her grandfather Nataniel Mayer, the first Lord Rothschild, founded the British branch of the Jewish Rothschild family's banking empire. Her mother Roszika von Werthernstein came from the first Jewish household to be enobled in Hungary. As a child, Miriam spent happy hours at her grandparents' large Hungarian estate, studying the natural world with her father, Charles Rothschild, a noted and avid naturalist.

She often referred to those early years of bliss as the time when she fell in love with studying insects and animals. World War I put an abrupt end to Miriam's visits to Hungary. At the outbreak of fighting in 1914, Miriam's siblings and parents fled Hungary, finding the last seats in a third-class coach that would bring them west to the Belgian coast. At one point, Miriam's family, along with other terrified civilians and a group of drunken reserve soldiers, were forced off the train and walked through a forest in the middle of the night to reach another station. With little luggage and a dwindling supply of cash, Rozsika was reduced to asking a fellow passenger for a loan to buy food for her children. "This is the proudest moment of my life: never did I think that I should be asked to lend money to a Rothschild!" her fellow passenger replied.

Back in England, Miriam lived at first in a grand family house in London and later in Ashton Wold, the Rothschild's large country estate. She was privately educated by tutors, and enjoyed roaming her family's woods and fields, observing birds and animals. Her idyllic world was shattered in 1923 when she was fifteen years old: her father ended his own life, and in so doing brought much of Miriam's innocence and exuberance to a close, as well. She retreated into herself, and afterwards was more guarded and wary.

Her brother Victor rekindled Miriam's interest in learning and sense of fun and excitement in the world a few years later. On a visit back home from his boarding school in Harrow, he begged Miriam to help him dissect a frog. "I was so thrilled with what I found...I went straight back into zoology with a pair of scissors in my hand," she later recalled. (Miriam and Victor would one day become the only brother and sister who were both fellows of Britain's Royal Society, a prestigious organization dedicated to furthering knowledge about the natural world.)

Miriam never gained a formal academic degree, but in her twenties she ran a research station in the southern English city of Plymouth, exploring ways of creating chicken food out of sustainable seaweed. She traveled widely, and on her many visits to continental Europe became alarmed at the rise of fascism and anti-Semitism. In 1938, when a museum official asked Miriam to take part in a new project - an activity she formerly might have had a hard time resisting - she demurred. "I am sorry to say that I am terribly busy…it is this question of (Jewish) refugees. Since the Anschluss I have been unable to do my scientific work…"

Terrified by the plight of Europe's Jews - including their many relatives in Hungary, France, and Germany - Miriam and her mother embarked on an intense schedule of speaking engagements in London and Plymouth, trying to raise awareness of the plight of European Jews and to galvanize support for welcoming Jewish refugees, particularly children. They welcomed Jewish orphans into Ashton Wold, eventually housing about fifty Jewish children there during World War II.

On a visit home to Ashton Wold in 1940, Miriam was sitting with her mother Roszika when Roszika suddenly died from a heart attack. This traumatic horror came in the midst of what was already an intensely stressful and unhappy time for Miriam: with the outbreak of the war, Miriam and had been recruited to work at Bletchley Park, the top-secret country home where a crack team of codebreakers worked round the clock to break Nazi Germany's "unbreakable" Enigma code. Miriam was part of a team of gifted women who worked the overnight shift, transcribing encoded Russian messages and translating items from German to English. She hated the pace and the stress, but with so much at stake there was no way that Miriam could resign from this essential job. Her mother's death rendered Miriam even more alone and isolated, trapped in a post that seemed too important to the war effort to give up, and more alone than before as she continued to push against England's establishment, urging her countrymen to accept more Jewish refugees.

She escaped whenever she could. Instead of sleeping in the Bletchley Park dormitories, Miriam drove each night to the nearby country estate of her friend, Lord Harry Rosebury, who kept a small apartment ready for her. She also began spending more time in Ashton Wold, and offered the use of her family's estate to the British and American armies. Soon, over 5,000 American soldiers, a military hospital, a contingent of British soldiers, and several dozen Jewish refugee children were living in Miriam's childhood home. Miriam leased a cottage in the nearby village of Ashton Wold for her personal use, and opened this home, too, to the war effort, providing refreshments and a place to rest and socialize to soldiers who were stationed in the area.

Much of Miriam's grand house was converted into a military hospital. One day in 1942, the matron of the hospital came to see Miriam. A British lieutenant who'd been wounded in action was in the hospital; he'd worked with Miriam's mother Roszika, helping bring Jewish children out of Nazi Germany in the 1930s, and was shocked to hear of Roszika's death. He was asking now if he might meet her daughter. Miriam demurred but the matron told Miriam something else: the lieutenant was devastatingly handsome. Miriam decided to go ahead and meet her mother's former colleague.

The meeting would change the course of Miriam's life. It also opened a window into another top secret British wartime initiative whose existence remained a secret for years: the "X Troop," a group of European Jewish soldiers who'd adopted British names and disguises and had been trained to be one of the British army's most crack commando units, sent to fight Nazis in Germany, France, and Italy.

X Troop was the brainchild of Lord Mountbatten, a member of Britain's royal family and a senior military commander who'd been directing Britain's special forces. In 1942, with Germany ascendant and the Allies in retreat, he suggested that Britain create a completely new unit drawn from European refugees whose deep-rooted hatred of Hitler - and fluency in German and other European languages - would ensure that they could be used for undercover intelligence work and for interrogating Nazi troops, as well as for fighting.

British Prime Minister Winston Churchill gave the new secret unit its name: "Because they will be unknown warriors...they must perforce be considered an unknown quantity. Since the algebraic symbol for the unknown is X, let us call them X Troop," he declared. In the end, 87 men, at least 82 of whom were Jews, made it through intense training and were selected to form the elite unit.

One of the soldiers was George Lane, born Lanyi Gyorgy into a Jewish family in Hungary. He'd worked as a journalist in Britain in the 1930's and partnered with Roszika Rothschild helping rescue Jewish orphans. In X Troop, he was dropped behind enemy lines. On one mission, he parachuted into occupied France with a collection of carrier pigeons. "It was pitch dark and I had to jump 400 feet into enemy territory. I landed in a field with the pigeons in a small cage strapped onto my chest. The goal was for them to deliver a secret message." He broke his arm and recuperated in the Ashton Wold hospital. Dashing, handsome, brilliant and brave, George won Miriam's heart and they married in a small ceremony in 1943.

Miriam moved with George to X Troop's base in the small Welsh town of Aberdovey. George's fellow soldiers used to jokingly call George the "Hungarian Hunk". Now they dubbed Miriam "The Lady of X Troop." They wisecracked that with George's good looks and Miriam's brilliance, their children would surely be perfect.

"You don't expect groups of soldiers to spend their time talking about Schopenhauer, about philosophy, but that's the sort of stuff we discussed the whole time," Miriam later recalled of her happy months in Wales with the X Troop soldiers. "They were very intellectual." She used her wealth and connections to obtain extra equipment and food rations for the soldiers.

In Wales, Miriam also developed a new area of scientific research: wood pigeons. She kept crates of pigeons under her bed. One day, alarmed by the pigeons and also by Miriam's code books, her landlady called the police and Miriam was arrested as a spy. In a huge coincidence, the report on her suspicious activities wound up on the desk of Miriam's brother Victor, who was working in military intelligence. He obtained her release, and asked her how she'd wound up in a small town in rural Wales with boxes of pigeons under her bed. Unable to divulge any secrets about X Troop or her codebreaking work, Miriam simply answered him: "What a lot of people are doing these days - following in the footsteps of true love."

Miriam found herself left alone for long periods as X Troop soldiers were deployed in some of the most dangerous fighting in Europe. George Lane took part in one of X Troop's greatest military triumphs, Operation Tarbrush, in April 1944. With the D-Day landings scheduled for June, it was crucial that the Allies had information about German defenses, particularly the powerful anti-personnel mines they'd deployed on France's Normandy coast. George and a British captain were selected for the mission.

After relaying the information back to the Allies, George and his comrade were captured by Nazi soldiers. In his prison cell, George was told to wash up because he was going to be interrogated by an important person. To his utter shock, he was taken into a room containing Field Marshal Rommel, Commander of Germany's *Wehrmacht*. "You realize that you are in a very tricky situation here, Lt. Lane?" the senior Nazi asked him. George realized that any slip that revealed he was actually a Hungarian Jew would be fatal.

Somehow, George kept his composure. Rommel spoke at length: Britain and Germany should be fighting on the same side, Rommel suggested: Communist Russia was the natural enemy to both countries.

Risking death, George could no longer keep quiet. "Sir, how can the British and Germans fight side by side, considering what we know about what the Nazis are doing to the Jews? No Englishman could ever tolerate such a thing." Rommel stared at him angrily but didn't react. After some more strained conversation, George was released. Later on, he managed to give the Allies crucial information about the location of Rommel's offices, materially helping the Allies in their D-Day plans.

With the conclusion of the war, Miriam and her family received the crushing news that many of their European relatives had been murdered by the Nazis. Her beloved Aunt Aranka had been beaten to death with meat hooks as soon as she arrived at Buchenwald concentration camp. Faced with such horror, Miriam found a powerful new cause to press: the inhumane conditions in which Allied soldiers were keeping Jewish survivors in the very same concentration camps they'd just liberated. Miriam lobbied government officials to improve treatment of Jewish survivors. Later on, she vigorously lobbied to help Jewish Holocaust survivors reclaim lost property. "The end of hostilities did not terminate the misery and desolation of the few central European Jews who had miraculously survived the Nazi holocaust or brutal forced labor," she wrote in one of her many papers on the subject. She continued to help Jewish survivors reclaim lost property for decades, never tiring of her political work and never losing the angry spark that drove her to demand justice.

After the war, Miriam and George moved to Ashton Wold. George farmed, Miriam continued her research, and they built a family. Miriam suffered two miscarriages which affected her deeply: eventually, they were able to have four living children. Mismatched in peacetime and dissatisfied, Miriam and George first moved to Oxfordshire, then divorced in 1957. They remained on good terms, and Miriam befriended George's second wife Elizabeth, whom he married in 1963.

Miriam continued her scientific research, focusing on fleas and cataloging the many species her father had collected. She also took up a number of progressive causes. In 1954 she joined an official commission arguing vociferously against the criminalization of homosexuality. After several of her friends died by suicide, she felt enormous guilt at not helping them more. When Miriam's very good friend, Gabrielle Fischer, took her own life, Miriam adopted Gabrielle's two children. Raising six children as a single mother was difficult, but Miriam laughed off her intense stress.

When Miriam's sister Liberty was diagnosed with Schizophrenia in 1959, Miriam and her cousin Evelyn founded the Schizophrenia Research Fund to encourage research into the disease, donating the staggering sum of 50,000 pounds from their family fortune. After a visit to Israel in 1961, Miriam became an outspoken critic of environmental destruction in Israel and called for awareness and conservation there. Back home at Ashton Wold, she established a protected nature reserve. She fought for free milk for children, better treatment for farm animals, and, after being inspired on a visit to the United States, advised Prince Charles on the benefits of planting wildflowers along the sides of highways.

Miriam's work as a naturalist catapulted her to heights of British research. Even though she never gained a formal university degree, in time she amassed eight honorary doctorates. Her magnum opus was her six-volume catalog of flea specimens, which took thirty years to complete. Miriam became one of the leading authorities on the chemical ecology of insects and did groundbreaking research on toxicity in plants. She was the first person to understand that rabbits' hormone cycles affected not only their own breeding cycles, but also those of the fleas living as parasites in their fur.

Miriam was the first female member of the Committee for Conservation of the National Trust and the first female trustee of the British Museum of Natural History. In her long life she amassed many honors, was granted the title Dame in 2000, and published over 300 scientific papers.

Miriam used to tell people that she wasn't religious. "I don't believe in God. But I do believe very strongly in the Jewish community. I don't mind who I say I'm Jewish to," she once told a journalist. Yet in her later life, she began to keep the Jewish Sabbath, refraining from working on Saturdays. It wasn't a traditional observance of the Jewish day of rest, but for Miriam Rothschild, whose life was a constant churn of work and research and collaboration and activity, the decision not to work on Shabbat was surprising, and a powerful statement that in the vast natural universe which she so loved and reveled in, there might still be room for God.

Hannah Senesh
1921 - 1944

"The only thing I'm committed to, in which I believe, is Zionism." Hannah Senesh
(spelled Szenes in Hungarian) wrote those lines in her diary in 1939, just months
before the outbreak of World War II. After a carefree childhood full of material
comforts and academic success, Hannah's world was darkening.

Her father, Bela Senesh, was a famous author. After he died when Hannah was
eight years old, Hannah and her brother Gyuri were raised by their doting mother
Catherine. The family was accorded deference on account of their famous father,
but throughout Hannah's teenage years, growing anti-Semitism convinced her that
Jews had no future in Hungary. She made no secret of her plans to move to the
land of Israel and join a Zionist pioneer collective farm.

Hannah was preternaturally gifted and charismatic, headstrong and determined.
When she graduated from high school with the highest marks possible, her mother
recalled, many of Hannah's teachers tried to convince her to stay in Hungary and
go to university. "Perhaps I ought to be impressed that in view of graduating
summa cum laude, and with a plethora of recommendations from teachers and
friends, I can get into the university, while a Gentile who just barely squeezed
through the exams can sail in!" Hannah told her mother. "Don't they understand

that I don't want to be just a student; that I have plans, dreams, ambitions; and that the road to their fulfillment would only be barred to me here?"

In 1939, Hannah moved to Mandatory Palestine: she studied in the agricultural college in Nahal for two years, then joined Kibbutz Sdot Yam near Caesarea. It should have been a happy time, yet World War II was then raging in Europe, and Hannah was tormented by what was taking place in her old home. She kept a diary - today it's a classic of Israeli literature - and she recorded the creeping dread of those years. In one 1940 passage, she describes her horror when British soldiers turned away a ship of desperate Jewish refugees that had somehow made it to the coast of Haifa. "The entire Jewish community (in Palestine) unanimously demanded that they be allowed to remain in the Land. But the ship sailed (away) during the night... What is there to add? What can we feel as human beings, as a people? And the question arises, How much longer?"

Her diary records the brutal toll of the war as one country in Europe after another fell to the Nazis. When it became impossible for her to send letters home to her beloved mother in Budapest any more, Hannah knew she had to do something, anything, to help the Allies. "Sometimes I feel I am an emissary who has been entrusted with a mission. What this mission is - is not clear to me."

Hannah joined the elite Jewish military organization *Palmach* and trained in radio operation and parachuting, yet she didn't put her military training to use - yet. By 1943, she was beside herself with worry about the Jewish family and friends she'd left behind, and resolved to return to Hungary somehow. "I'm quite aware how absurd the idea is," she recorded; "It still seems both feasible and necessary to me, so I'll get to work on it and carry it through."

Just a few weeks later, Yonah Rosen, another young *Palmach* member from Hungary, visited Hannah's kibbutz with just the proposition she'd been waiting for: the British army was assembling a team of volunteers to parachute into Nazi-occupied Europe in order to help Allied efforts organize local anti-Nazi resistance movements. They were looking for soldiers from European countries so that they could blend in with the populace without arousing suspicion. Would Hannah like to volunteer?

"I was truly astounded: the *identical* idea! My answer, of course, was that I'm absolutely ready," she wrote in her journal. "I see the hand of destiny in this, just as I did at the time of my Aliyah. I wasn't master of my fate then either. I was enthralled by one idea, and it gave me no rest: I knew I would emigrate, despite the many obstacles in my path. Now I again sense the excitement of something important and vital ahead and the feeling of inevitability connected with a decisive and urgent step."

Preparations took months. Finally, in 1944, Hannah, along with 32 other Jewish soldiers, was dropped into Nazi-controlled Yugoslavia. The group hid their true mission of helping organize Jewish resistance and presented themselves to resistance leader Josip Broz Tito's partisan fighters as British reinforcements. They fought in Yugoslavia for three months. Ever the center of attention, a beacon of idealism to all who encountered her, Hannah charmed the resistance fighters in Yugoslavia. "She became something of a legend," recalled Reuven Dafne, another *Palmach* recruit who fought alongside Hannah in Yugoslavia.

He described Hannah's reaction in March 1944 when she and the other partisans heard the news that Nazi Germany had occupied Hungary: "it was the first time I saw Hannah cry...amidst her sobs she exclaimed, 'What will happen to all of them...to the million Jews in Hungary? They're in German hands now - and we're sitting here...just sitting.'"

The *Palmach* soldiers were desperate to get to Hungary, but with the border closed it was incredibly difficult. Eventually, on June 9, 1944, both Reuven Dafne and Hannah managed to cross battlefields and reach the border of Hungary: they agreed that Hannah would enter the country first, leaving Reuven in the relative safety of Yugoslavia, so that he could carry on their mission if she fell. "We shook hands and thanked each other for shared experiences," Reuven recalled. Hannah pressed a scrap of paper into Reuven's hand, then disappeared around a bend in the road. It was the last time he would ever see her. When he opened the paper she'd given him, he saw it was a Hebrew poem Hannah had penned soon after landing in Yugoslavia:

Blessed is the Match

Blessed is the match consumed in kindling flame.
Blessed is the flame that burns in the secret fastness of the heart.
Blessed is the heart with strength to stop its beating for honor's sake.
Blessed is the match consumed in kindling flame.

(Translated by Elie Leshem.)

Hannah rendezvoused inside Hungary with four other *Palmach* fighters. Together, they made their way through thick forests with only basic maps and a compass to guide them. They carried parts of a radio transmitter with them, which they planned to set up once they'd established a base. Tragically, they never got the chance. Two of the fighters were arrested by Hungarian gendarmes, who found the radio transmitter pieces. Soon, Hannah and the fourth fighter were arrested, too.

They were taken to a local police station, where Hannah was brutally beaten for three days: the torture rendered her shattered, with teeth missing, and her body covered with bruises and wounds. Afterwards, she was transferred to a Gestapo prison in Budapest, the city where her mother was still living.

At that very moment, Hannah's mother, Catherine, was preparing to emigrate to the Land of Israel. Hannah's brother Gyuri was finally in Israel, and Catherine was awaiting false papers that would allow her to follow her children there: she was overjoyed that her small family would soon be reunited. Her joy was broken, however, when SS soldiers appeared at her door early one morning, and brought her in for questioning.

A Gestapo official asked Catherine about her children. Puzzled, she answered his questions, particularly about her daughter Hannah, whom she described as brilliant and accomplished. Asked where Hannah was at that moment, Catherine proudly pointed to the Land of Israel on a large map of the world hanging in the room. She was shocked when the official suddenly announced that Hannah was, in fact, in the neighboring room. He ordered Hannah to be brought in.

"Four men led her in," Catherine recalled later. "Had I not known she was coming, perhaps in that first moment I would not have recognized the Hannah of five years ago. Her once soft, wavy hair hung in a filthy tangle, her ravaged face reflected untold suffering, her large, expressive eyes were blackened, and there were ugly welts on her cheeks and neck…"

Catherine was arrested, too, and held for three months in the same prison, which was filled not with criminals but with Jewish women. At times she could see Hannah, who was kept in solitary confinement for much of the time, with the exceptions of nearly daily interrogations, during which she was often tortured. Even in prison, Hannah's effusive personality affected everyone around her. When she was allowed to mix with the general prison population, she befriended Jewish orphans in the jail, teaching them to read and write, singing them songs and telling them stories, and making beautiful dolls for them out of scraps of rags and strings. "She thought of things to occupy the adults too, and entertained them with anecdotes and songs about Palestine," her mother recalled.

During her periods in solitary confinement, Hannah communicated with the rest of the prisoners by cutting out large letters from paper and displaying them in her cell's tiny window. Hannah was often the best informed in the prison due to her frequent interrogations in Gestapo headquarters, where she overheard scraps of conversation, and she became a source of news about the outside world. One day Hannah spied her mother wearing a yellow Jewish star through her window and, using cutout letters, asked what it meant. When her mother explained, Hannah drew a Jewish star in the dirt on her window too: it remained there for weeks.

Hannah was charged with treason and brought to trial at the end of October 1944. The Judge Advocate in her trial, Captain Julian Simon, found her guilty and sentenced her to death. With the end of the war in sight, the Judge Advocate's office had all but declared that it wouldn't carry out the execution. Yet Hannah's very passion and eloquence throughout her trial aroused a renewed and vicious hatred amongst the Hungarian officials.

Records of her trial have been destroyed, but some eyewitnesses recreated much of what she said there. Hannah spoke about her love for Hungary when she was a child, and how the slow realization that, as a Jew, she had no future in Hungary dampened her youthful idealism. She spoke about Hungary's bitter alliance with Nazi Germany and how this was a betrayal of all that was good. After the judge interjected that she was a traitor, Hannah replied that he and other Hungarian officials were the true traitors. She implored him not to add to the terrible injustices Hungary had already seen.

The war would soon end, Hannah told Capt. Simon and the rest of the court; when it did, every Jew who remained alive in Hungary would become a judge, evaluating Hungary's actions. Don't add to the sins of the country by condemning me to death, she pleaded.

Her impassioned speech merely infuriated Capt. Simon. Later on, he visited her cell and demanded that she beg for mercy. Hannah refused, and Capt. Simon, in a fit of pique, ordered her execution for one hour from then. He said she could write farewell letters, and strode out of her cell.

An hour later, Hannah was led into a snowy courtyard to face death by firing squad. She refused a blindfold, staring defiantly at her murderers as she died. Her mother was told of her murder afterwards, and given Hannah's final letter: "Dearest Mother, I don't know what to say - only this, a million thanks, and forgive me if you can. You know so well why words aren't necessary. With love forever, Your daughter"

After her death, the following poem was found in Hannah's prison cell:

One - Two - Three

One - two - three...
Eight feet wide
Two strides end to end, dismal dark.
Life but a fading question mark.

One - two - three…
Maybe a week more,
By month end, will I be dead,
Death hangs low, overhead.

I would be twenty-three
This July.
I gambled, damned be the cost,
The die was cast. - I lost.

(Translated by Joe Varadi.)

Julian Simon, who ordered her execution, moved to Argentina after the war. When he was 74, he was asked about Hannah Senesh's death.: "If I were to start my life over, I would have chosen again to become a military judge and would have sentenced her to death again," he answered defiantly.

Hannah was buried in the Jewish cemetery in Budapest, but then reinterred in Jerusalem in 1950. The many letters, poems and songs she wrote throughout her short, impassioned life are treasured in Israel today.

Tosia Altman
1922 - 1943

The unofficial song of the Jewish Ghetto fighters during World War II, *Zog nit keyn mol* ("Never Say," written by partisan fighter Hirsh Glick, 1922-1944) declares in one of its stanzas that:

This song is written with blood, and not with pencil.
It's not a tune sung by birds in the wild.
This song was sung by people amidst collapsing walls,
Sung with pistols in their hands.

The Jewish fighters so described are a sadly overlooked part of history. As Nazis consolidated their rule over Europe, they established over a thousand Ghettos in towns and cities they'd conquered in which to imprison, enslave, deport and kill millions of Jews, as well as many thousands of Roma. Conditions were abysmal and those who didn't succumb to starvation and rampant disease were deported to Nazi death camps. The largest of these ghettos were in Poland: the Warsaw Ghetto housed nearly half a million Jews; the Lodz Ghetto contained over 200,000 Jews.

At least 90 of these Ghettos had armed Jewish resistance units. History writer Judy Batalion estimates that approximately 30,000 European Jews joined these partisans. "Rescue networks supported about 12,000 Jews in hiding in Warsaw alone," she notes; "All this alongside daily acts of resilience - smuggling food,

166

writing diaries, telling a joke to relieve fear, hugging a barrack mate to keep her warm. Women, aged 16 to 25, were at the helm of many of these efforts." One of the most active of these many women was Tosia Altman, a vivacious young woman from the central Polish city of Wloclawek who was twenty when World War II broke out in 1939.

Tosia's family was an oasis of culture and education within intense anti-Semitism. Tosia was a sensitive child, afraid of dogs and fearful of the dark. Her family home was filled with books, and her family frequently discussed their commitment to building a Jewish homeland in the Land of Israel. Yet her childhood was roiled by anti-Semitic violence and fear. Once, when she was young, she heard a pogrom raging outside, the nighttime silence rent by screams from terrified Jews and barking dogs. In order to conquer her fears, Tosia forced herself to go outside, hearing these terrible sounds and proving to herself that she could withstand them.

As a teenager, Tosia joined the popular Socialist Zionist youth movement *Hashomer Ha'Tzair* and rose in the ranks, eventually becoming leader of her local branch. Her friends remembered her as bubbly and outgoing. She hated disagreements and tried to be a peacemaker; she also was flirtatious, with many friends and boyfriends. After attending the group's Fourth World Convention when she was sixteen, Tosia made the momentous decision to move to the Land of Israel. She moved to a training kibbutz in southern Poland to learn how to farm. In 1938, the organization appointed Tosia head of youth education in Warsaw; the move must have seemed like an honor at the time, but it had the unintended consequence of trapping Tosia in Europe when war broke out.

After western Poland was overrun by Nazi forces in September, 1939, *Hashomer Ha'Tzair* ordered their leaders to move eastward, to Russian-occupied areas where Jews were safer. Tosia and her fellow young leaders made their way - partially on foot, and at times through fighting and bombing - to Vilna, Lithuania, where they hoped to regroup and leave Europe for the Land of Israel. After many unsuccessful attempts to find transport, they were forced to abandon their plans.

Instead, *Hashomer Ha'Tzair* had a daunting new mission for Tosia. Since she was blonde, pretty and outgoing, it seemed that she might succeed in passing as a non-

Jew. Would she return to German-occupied Poland and organize Jewish youth group members to resist the Nazis? Privately, Tosia despaired and cried to her friends: giving up her dearly held plans to move to the Land of Israel was incredibly painful. Yet Tosia was also a committed *Hashomer Ha'Tzair* member and agreed right away to undertake this daring mission.

Jews were no longer allowed to travel on trains in Nazi-occupied Poland, but Tosia disguised herself as a non-Jewish Polish woman and traveled between the Jewish Ghettos that were being established. In Warsaw, she and other youth group leaders set up educational programs and a newspaper to help sustain the spirit of the Jews imprisoned there. She corresponded with other *Hashomer Ha'Tzair* leaders for a time, writing in code. Soon, however, sending messages became impossible.

Historian Ziva Shalev has noted that once Warsaw's Jews were confined in the Warsaw Ghetto in November 1940, Tosia's "blonde hair and fluent Polish were no longer enough; with every trip, she risked death. Forged papers, outdated documents and stamps, and the danger of Polish informants who 'sniffed out' Jews were all a constant peril. But Altman continued to travel (throughout the region), her visits serving as a source of strength and encouragement to the young people." Imprisoned inside hellish Ghettos, the appearance of a free Jewish woman - an emissary from an official Zionist group no less - must have felt overwhelming.

Writer Judy Batalion combed accounts of Tosia's visits. Again and again, Jews in Polish Ghettos recorded "'the day that Tosia arrived' in their ghettos. Her appearance was like an injection of sunshine into their dark lives - a 'jolt of electric energy.' People did not sense her ambivalent interior; they rejoiced, cried, and hugged her close. She brought warmth, 'inexhaustible optimism,' a sense of connectedness, the relief at not being forgotten, the feeling that things might somehow be okay."

When news of the systematic slaughter of Jews began to reach *Hashomer Ha'Tzair* leadership, Tosia's mission changed: she continued to travel throughout Poland, but now warned Jews that the Nazis were carrying out genocide. Nothing less than the complete elimination of the Jewish community seemed to be their goal. In 1942, when the first large-scale deportation of Jews began from the Warsaw

Ghetto, Tosia and other youth group leaders helped start the *Żydowska Organizacja Bojowa* (ZOB), the "Jewish Fighting Organization," to facilitate armed resistance.

Once again, relying on her non-Jewish looks and her charismatic personality, Tosia smuggled herself in and out of the Warsaw Ghetto, coordinating with the two main Polish resistance organizations, the nationalist *Armia Krajowa* (AK) and the Communist group *Armia Ludowa*. Her goal was to obtain donations of arms to help Jews fight within the Warsaw Ghetto. She managed to smuggle guns and grenades through the Polish countryside, hiding the arms in her clothes, and smuggle them into the Warsaw and Krakow Ghettos. At one point, in 1943, Tosia was arrested, but managed to escape her Nazi prison with the help of a *Hashomer Ha'Tzair* comrade, and continued to fight. Concerned that her hiding places had been compromised, Tosia moved into the Warsaw Ghetto and worked with the young leaders there who were preparing to mount a large-scale offensive against the Nazis.

When the Warsaw Ghetto uprising broke out on April 18, 1943, Tosia was in the thick of the fighting. Her job was to relay information within the Ghetto and also to the outside world. She also helped smuggle Jews out of the Ghetto through sewers. After three weeks of fighting, Tosia and a few other survivors managed to escape the Ghetto through sewers themselves. They hid in the attic of a celluloid factory in Warsaw. On the night of May 24, 1943, when Tosia was twenty three years old, her hiding place caught fire. Tosia was badly injured and either jumped from or fell off the factory's roof. Severely injured, she was arrested by Polish officers who promptly turned her over to Nazi officials. Tosia was tortured and died two days later, in agony, in Nazi custody.

Bella Abramovna
1937 - 1982

When Bella Abramovna was six, someone gave her a middle school math book. It was a huge volume with thousands of mathematical problems: Bella had solved them all within a month.

Bella's father died fighting Hitler when Bella was just a child; she grew up in a tiny apartment in Moscow with her mother. Although Jewish education and religious rituals were banned in the Soviet Union, Bella's mother passed on to Bella a clear knowledge of her Jewish identity. When she was young, this meant speaking Yiddish with her family and later her husband and enjoying Jewish folk tunes. As Bella grew up, she was reminded of her Jewishness another way: through relentless prejudice and insults. Faced with crippling anti-Semitism, Bella decided to fight back, defying the Soviet Union's repression of its Jews. She is one of Russian Jewry's greatest heroes; her remarkable life deserves to be remembered.

After Stalin's death in 1953, the USSR's Jews enjoyed a brief period of tolerance. It was during this time, in 1955, that Bella graduated high school and decided to study both math and music in university. Gifted in both subjects, Bella was accepted to the prestigious Mechanics and Mathematics Faculty of Moscow State University and the renowned Gnessinykh Musical Institute. She flourished, writing mathematical papers and emerging as a major thinker.

She met her husband Ilya Muchnik in 1960 when they both attended a seminar on the use of math in music. He later recalled that "we wandered through university corridors and discussed various possibilities of computer-generated music." But it wasn't Ilya's intellectual prowess that drew Bella to him; she enjoyed the freedom that came from spending time with another Jewish student. "She suddenly understood that with me she could sit, listen and understand songs that were of great interest to her. Computer capabilities concerned her little. She just immersed herself in Jewish folk melody," Ilya later recalled.

The two married the following year and settled in a heavily Jewish suburb outside of Moscow where all their neighbors spoke Yiddish like them. Bella worked on her Ph.D., publishing major breakthroughs in mathematics, and gave birth to her daughter Masha. Since there were no outlets for adult education in their little suburb, a neighbor started teaching math to curious adults who wanted to expand their intellectual horizons, and Bella volunteered her time teaching alongside her. Once Masha was born, Bella turned her attention to tutoring young children in math instead, instructing them and also tutoring students for the difficult entrance exams to the math departments in Russia's prestigious universities.

This tutoring gave Bella a close up view of the doors that were fast slamming shut in the faces of the Soviet Union's Jews. Schools like Moscow State University, where Bella had studied, were now only admitting a tiny handful of Jews. Jews who wished to study math and other subjects could only do so by applying to far-flung universities in Siberia; many gave up on their dreams of university-level study altogether.

Bella was friends with the Russian Jewish researcher Boris Kanevsky, who was documenting this discrimination. He described the plight of Russian Jewish students as "Intellectual Genocide:" an entire generation of Jewish students was being denied an education and any outlet for their intellectual potential.

In the 1970s, Bella and Ilya divorced and Bella and her daughter Masha moved into a small two-room apartment in Moscow. Faced with intense anti-Jewish discrimination all around her, Bella decided to do something to fight back. In 1978, she defied the Soviet authorities and announced to Moscow's Jewish population that for the first time in a generation, Jewish children would be able to study high-level, college math. She opened a clandestine school in her home and proudly named it "The Jewish People's University."

It was an incredibly risky move. The Soviet authorities were ruthless in finding and punishing expressions of Jewish identity. Everything not controlled by the USSR was subject to sudden closure. Bella - as well as the Jewish students she instructed and the Jewish mathematicians she recruited to teach - were running a grave risk by studying outside of established universities.

Nevertheless, Jews flocked to her Jewish "University".

The school opened in 1978 with 14 students and two lecturers. Within the first month, 30 students were attending classes. By the end of 1979, there were 110 students. Bella's apartment was so tiny that the large chalkboard she bought for lessons had to be brought in through a window as it wouldn't fit up the rickety staircase to her home. Bella quickly realized that if she was to teach all the Jewish students in Moscow who were hungry to learn, she'd have to expand into different premises. She arranged for classes to be given on the weekends in local universities when their lecture halls were empty. She personally would stop by the lectures, delivering handmade sandwiches to students and teachers.

Mathematician Andrei Zelevinsky taught at Bella's "university" and he later recalled that "her warmth, kindness, and optimism immediately made one predisposed towards her and feel at ease with her. She showed motherly affection to the Jewish People's University's students and... evoked equally warm feelings in response. The organization of the Jewish People's University demanded of her great courage and resolve...but there was no sign of self-importance or 'showing off.'" For a few years, the Jewish People's University flourished.

Andrei Zeelvinsky reminisced: "Bella Abramovna's...idea was humane and simple: attempt to at least partially restore fairness by offering students who were seriously interested in mathematics the possibility of receiving that fundamental mathematical education which the administrators of (prestigious schools like Moscow State University) deprived them."

From the very beginning, the school was infiltrated by KGB agents. Bella gave stern instructions: only math could ever be discussed. She hoped that by avoiding any political conversation the authorities would leave her students and instructors alone. For five years the KGB waited, biding their time, allowing classes to continue. Hundreds of students passed through the "university" in that time. They received no official degrees, but an education that they never could have otherwise hoped for. For a generation of students, Bella's Jewish People's University was their only way to avoid the "intellectual genocide" that encompassed generations of Jewish students in the Soviet Union who were denied access to higher education.

In 1982, the KGB finally moved against the school. Two of the teachers Bella had recruited were arrested and accused of working against the state. Soon, Bella herself was called into KGB headquarters. She gave a statement about her activities and was released. Over the next few days she was called into KGB headquarters again and again, charged with operating a Jewish People's University outside of the law. Bella calmly explained her activities over and over, insisting that she was merely providing lessons for students and had done nothing wrong.

Her final interrogation came on September 24, 1982. After being released from KGB headquarters, Bella went to visit her mother. She left her mother's Moscow apartment at around 11 o'clock at night and was walking home along a quiet street when a car slowly passed her by. It seemed that the people inside were staring at her, perhaps to identify her. Soon after that a speeding truck barreled down the quiet lane, hitting Bella. As she lay in a heap on the ground, another car drove up to her lifeless body, paused beside her, then drove off. Almost immediately, an ambulance came and took Bella to the morgue. She was 44 years old.

Bella was buried the next day. Her death bore all the hallmarks of a KGB hit and nobody dared to speak at her funeral. Bella Abramovna (she was also sometimes called Bella Subbotovskaya) was a famous mathematician, yet in death few people had the courage to speak up for her memory.

One mourner, Katherine Tylevich, recalled the fear that marked Bella's burial: "Her funeral was a silent one. Amidst (Bella) Subbotovskaya's students, colleagues, friends, family, and admirers, stood several unwelcome guests - several members of the KGB. Nobody volunteered to eulogize her; nobody made a sound except for her mother. The elderly Rebecca Yevseyevna (Bella's mother) finally cried out: 'Why won't anybody pronounce one word!?' Bella's...husband quickly escorted the aged woman out of the funeral home."

Bella Abramovna is today remembered as a pioneering mathematician for her work on logic and computational complexity theory. In addition to her research, she deserves to be remembered as a forgotten Jewish hero, too. Her Jewish People's University enriched the lives of hundreds of Jewish students, sustaining them during the darkest days of Soviet discrimination and repression.

Pamela Cohen

born 1943

Dismissed time and again as a nobody, "just a housewife," Pam helped thousands of Soviet Jews in their struggles to live Jewish lives and for the right to emigrate to Israel and the United States. She became one of the most important figures in the long struggle to help Soviet Jews - while remaining largely ignored and underestimated by many of the so-called "leaders" who claimed to speak for global Jewry.

Growing up in a quiet Chicago suburb, Pam's family wasn't particularly observant, though her parents always stressed the importance of Jewish community. "They instilled in me the value that you are responsible for your people. You have a duty to help others who are in danger," she explained.

After marrying her husband Lenny, living in the upscale suburb of Deerfield, and raising their three young children, political activism was the last thing on Pam's mind. That all changed one evening in June, 1970 when Pam and Lenny watched the evening news and heard the remarkable story about a group of Soviet Jews who'd been arrested for trying to hijack a plane to bring them to the West. "We couldn't wrap our heads around it," Pam says. "Jewish hijackers?"

Jews faced persistent, widespread discrimination across the Soviet Union. Jews were denied entry to prestigious universities. They were identified by their religion on their Soviet ID cards and faced persecution. If any Jew wished to learn more about his or her heritage and practice their religion, the reprisals were swift.

Teaching Hebrew was forbidden. Owning Jewish books was cause for arrest. The few synagogues that were allowed to exist were hotbeds of KGB espionage. The entire apparatus of the vast Soviet state was mobilized to crush any stirrings of Jewish identity and pride.

Yet they couldn't succeed entirely. Thousands of Soviet Jews resisted in ways large and small, determined to live Jewish lives.

In her memoirs, *Hidden Heroes: One Woman's Story of Resistance and Rescue in the Soviet Union*, Pam describes the electrifying effect that the 1967 Six-Day War between Israel and its Arab neighbors had on Jews in the Soviet Union. "The Soviet propagandists, on state-controlled television, repeatedly broadcast the onslaught of the Arab armies, thus signaling the imminent defeat of the fledgling Jewish state. On their television screens, Soviet Jews watched their brethren, proud uniformed Israeli soldiers, ready to die for a Jewish state – a national homeland where Jews weren't pariahs, where they could live with pride. Like a lightning bolt piercing the propaganda smokescreen, the cognitive recognition of a Jewish home gave Soviet Jews a new sense of peoplehood, dignity, and national purpose."

Soviet Jews began reading anything they could find to learn more about Israel and their Jewish religion. Leon Uris's 1958 novel *Exodus* was smuggled into the Soviet Union, where it was translated into Russian and laboriously copied by hand and distributed far and wide.

In 1970, a group of 16 young Jews hatched a daring plan to attract the attention of the West to the plight of Jews unable to leave the USSR. They bought tickets for all the seats on a 12-seat plane. They planned to hijack the plane, then fly the plane to Sweden. Once in freedom, they ultimately planned to go to Israel. As they feared, the KGB was on to their plan and intercepted them as they arrived at the airport on the morning of June 15, 1970. The group was put on trial and handed harsh sentences. Two of the young Jews were sentenced to death (these sentences were later changed to harsh prison terms); the rest were sentenced to years of imprisonment in harsh gulags in Siberia.

Reading their names and hearing about the determination of this group of brave young Jews was a turning point for Pam. "In a flash of recognition, I knew that

Yosef Mendelevich, Hillel Butman, Sylva Zalmanson, her husband Edward Kuznetsov, and the rest of this group were Jewish moral giants who had pitted themselves against the Kremlin. But I wanted to know more. Who were they? How had they come to make a decision that would result in years of imprisonment and hard labor in Siberia?"

In the ensuing weeks, Pam searched for news about the Jewish hijackers, and about Soviet Jews in general – and found very little information. Few people she knew in her heavily Jewish suburb knew about the terrible conditions of Soviet Jews, and few seemed to care. Many of the American Jews Pam knew seemed apathetic and indifferent to the grave danger some Jews faced around the world.

Not all American Jews were indifferent. A local woman phoned Pam and identified herself as a volunteer with a small organization called Chicago Action for Soviet Jewry, which lobbied politicians to raise awareness of the plight of Soviet Jews. She'd heard that Pam had an interest in Soviet Jews: would she consider helping sell commemorative cards to raise money for the organization? It was the invitation Pam had been waiting for. She joined the tiny group and spent her evenings learning about the intricacies of Soviet and American politics and lobbying American officials. Pam helped organize local Jews in Chicago to write letters to American politicians and to refuseniks (Jews who'd applied to emigrate from to Israel and been refused permission) in the Soviet Union.

The Chicago group was part of a larger umbrella organization, the Union of Councils for Soviet Jews, which coordinated the activities of a patchwork of activists across the United States, as well as in France, Britain and other countries. "I was shocked to discover that the task of saving millions of Soviet Jews was limited to a group of about thirty activists, grassroots volunteers who operated their local independent council in the United States, London or Paris. But these unsalaried activists projected an image of strength that vastly magnified the reality of their numbers."

Pam would eventually serve as a leader of Chicago Action for Soviet Jewry and then as national president of the Union of Councils for Soviet Jews. Throughout her years of activism, Pam remained intensely humble and focused on her many allies in the fight to help Soviet Jews. She never wanted to be seen as sweeping in from outside, telling Soviet Jews what to do or taking the credit for battles they were fighting from the inside. Indeed, in the memoir she wrote, she spends most of her pages documenting the names and lives of little-known refuseniks who spent years resisting the crushing might of the Soviet Union in any way they could.

There were the secret Hebrew teachers who risked arrest and exile by teaching their fellow Jews. Some Jews published and distributed secret Jewish newsletters and books. Many Soviet Jews insisted on embracing their Jewish traditions and lifestyles. Each one was an act of defiance.

Prisoners of conscience, known as *Zeks* in Russian, were Jews who went to prison for their beliefs and insistence on living an authentically Jewish life. Other Jews were wrongfully declared insane and sent to punitive psychiatric hospitals where they were subjected to horrific tortures, all in the name of "treatment" for their "insanity" of wishing to live in Israel. Pam saw herself as a partner to these brave souls, supporting their activities from afar.

At the Chicago Action for Soviet Jewry, Pam began documenting the case histories of every refusenik she could. In most cases, refuseniks were fired from their jobs. Unable to support themselves, they faced arrest for the crime of "parasitism." Countless more Jews found themselves unable to even file applications to emigrate – these Jews were sometimes called *waitniks*. Each refusenik had a file in Pam's office, with their individual circumstances and needs written down and shared with activists who would write letters to them, lobby politicians on their behalf, or even smuggle desperately needed goods to refuseniks inside the Soviet Union.

Sometimes huge coincidences helped Pam and her allies to send aid, giving her the distinct impression that their path was being eased somehow in uncanny ways. One of the Chicago Action for Soviet Jewry's most potent tools was activists who traveled to the Soviet Union as tourists in order to meet with refuseniks. Pam and her colleagues spent many long hours briefing these American travelers about the political situation in the USSR, the individual stories of the people they'd be meeting, and preparing them for the possibility of KGB arrest or interference.

When Pam once got a desperate phone call explaining that a refusenik needed emergency heart surgery and required an artificial heart valve, Pam soon heard about an American doctor who was planning to visit the Soviet Union who could bring this life-saving item with him. When Moscow refuseniks asked her to send an attorney for the legal defense of an arrested refusenik, she couldn't inform them on the KGB-monitored phone line that even as they were speaking, a top activist attorney was already in the air on his way to them in Moscow.

When word got to Pam that the famed refusenik Ida Nudel was being kept in horrific conditions in a Siberian gulag and was freezing, Pam records that "In the next tourist's suitcase was my sheepskin coat. The coat traveled from Chicago to Moscow to Siberia. I never knew how she knew it came from me, but after she was released, I received a letter from her, thanking me, and I framed it."

"The bear fat – that was the most remarkable coincidence," Pam recounted in a recent interview with a chuckle. When a well-known refusenik sent word to Pam that he needed bear fat for a folk remedy for a Chinese doctor to treat a recently released, badly beaten Jewish prisoner, Pam assumed this outlandish request would be impossible to honor. Pam didn't dismiss his request, but logistics simply made it impossible to obtain bear fat. "Who even heard of that in Chicago?" she recalled. "But our colleagues in Alaska did have access to bear fat and a businessman was about to depart from Alaska and agreed to take it to the refusenik's very city."

As years went by, Pam began to notice a jarring disconnect. She spent much of her days immersed in the struggles of Jews who were willing to risk their lives and freedom to have the chance to celebrate Jewish holidays or learn Hebrew or move to the Jewish State, yet Pam found herself living in assimilated, apathetic, Jewish suburbia.

One turning point came when Pam read a letter from a refusenik in Riga named Alexander Mariasin. In it, he told a heart-wrenching story about a group of Jews who insisted on celebrating the holiday of Simchat Torah even while they were trapped in a cattle car on their way to a Nazi death camp. "'It's a wonderful story,' Mariasin wrote in his letter, 'about a wonderful people. And so we celebrated Simchat Torah and were merry, too'," defying the Soviet authorities.

"Simchat Torah?" Pam wondered when she read those words. "How many of us in Deerfield took Simchat Torah seriously, or even knew what it was? The letter triggered in me a longing for something I never had, an inheritance that had disappeared somewhere on the boat between Lithuania or Poland and new lives here. The growth of the refuseniks was inspiring my own."

Pam was inspired by the courage and tenacity of famed refusenik Yosef Mendelevich, one of the hijackers in 1970. After his release from a harrowing 11 years in Siberian labor camps and prisons, he explained how he learned Hebrew in prison. Each day he wrote a word on a slip of paper and hid it in his belt, knowing that discovery by prison guards could incur a term in a solitary isolation cell. He suggested that Pam do the same. How could Pam ignore her own Jewish learning, she wondered, when she was faced with examples of men and women who took such risks just for the privilege of learning a single Hebrew word?

When dissident Hebrew teacher Ari (Leonid) Volvosky wrote to Pam to ask if she'd send him an English-language copy of the classic Jewish work *Book of Our Heritage* by Eliyahu Kitov, she complied, and bought a copy for herself as well. After that, Pam recalls, "every book that refuseniks asked for in English, I got a copy for myself."

Ari Volvovsky was sent to internal exile in Gorky. When Pam's son Scott celebrated his bar mitzvah, Volvovksy sent him a stirring letter that Pam includes in her book. "Today the...right to choose is before you," Volvovsky wrote. "One way is the way of Torah and commandments... The other is the way of growing apart from...Judaism. It is all in your hand and God will give you the strength and courage to choose the right way... On this important day, we should not forget our brothers and sisters who sacrificed their lives for the existence of our nation and for the establishment of our State, Israel... We should not forget our people in the Diaspora who cannot live in freedom, and it is our holy responsibility to help them with all our power."

This message hit home. Eventually Pam and Lenny set up a center for Jewish studies in their suburban home as their commitment to Jewish learning and practice deepened. Ever following the example of refuseniks, they purchased an apartment in Israel and ultimately made aliyah.

One of Pam's greatest frustrations in her work was the huge disconnect between Pam and her fellow activists and the relative indifference of many Jewish leaders inside mainstream Jewish institutions. Her role model was Peter Bergson, a Zionist leader in the 1940s who advocated for building a Jewish army to help rescue Jews in Nazi lands. Opposed by the Jewish establishment, Bergson nevertheless educated American Jews about the horrors taking place in Jewish communities behind Nazi lines.

Pam observed the same reluctance on the part of mainstream Jewish organizations to act on behalf of Soviet Jews. "When I became the national president of the Union of Councils for Soviet Jews, I felt like I wanted to put Bergson's mold on the organization. We weren't building an organization, we were building a strike force," she notes.

A typical example of her outsider tactics came late one night in the 1980s, when Pam got a phone call at home: a delegation of Soviet prosecutors was arriving in the morning; one of them had handed down terrible sentences of prison and lengthy stays in labor camps to Soviet Jews whose only crimes were wanting to emigrate or to learn more about their heritage. Unbelievably, instead of calling out their inhumanity, many Chicago Jews were planning to welcome the group. "They were coming at the invitation of the Chicago Bar Association to meet with the city's most prominent attorneys, including many Jews, who would wine and dine their celebrated guests," Pam wrote in her memoirs. "It was intolerable." She immediately got on the phone and organized a last-minute demonstration downtown outside of the location where the prosecutors were being feted.

When he was imprisoned in the Soviet Union, Natan Sharansky was shown a video by his captors of a demonstration on his behalf in the United States. "Do you see who is demonstrating for you?" his captors sneered at him: "nobodies - an army of students and housewives." Long after his release, Sharansky praised Pam's "army of students and housewives" who went to battle again and again, often in the face of indifference from much more powerful Jewish institutions, to aid their fellow Jews.

"We felt like there was a fire burning and we had to put it out. There was always way more to do than we could possibly do, and we just had to do all we could,"

Pam has explained. She hopes that her example inspires a new generation of Jews to embrace their own Jewish heritage. "You cannot know where you're going unless you know where you're from," she notes. "You're here for a reason and each of us has an obligation to work hard to make the world a much better place."

Devorah Halberstam
born 1957

In 2021, when the New York City Police Department announced the creation of a new Hate Crime Review Panel, its chair was an elegant, diminutive Jewish woman, Devorah Halberstam. For over a quarter century, Devorah has been a champion of tolerance and for battling hate crimes in New York and beyond.

Her career in law enforcement was sparked in 1994 by a horrific tragedy, when her beloved son, Ari, was brutally murdered in an anti-Jewish terror attack on New York's Brooklyn Bridge.

"Ari was my firstborn child," Devorah recalled in a phone conversation. "He was so good, so innocent." On March 1, 1994, Ari, 16, was traveling in a van with 14 other Jewish teenage boys. Lubavitch Chassidic Jews, the boys were dressed in a recognizably Jewish manner, making them targets in a brutal, planned anti-Semitic attack.

As they crossed over the Brooklyn Bridge, a Lebanese cab driver named Rashid Baz shot at the car, wounding four of the boys. Ari was rushed to the hospital and placed on a respirator, his prognosis grim. Two other boys, Nachum Sossonkin and Levi Wilhelm, were seriously injured and underwent major surgery. Ari later died from his wounds.

The gunman was arrested the next day and confessed to being the shooter. A jury later rejected his claim of insanity and convicted him of second-degree murder as well as 14 counts of attempted murder. Baz was sentenced to 141 years in prison.

Many people seemed to be willing to put the horrific case behind them, but Devorah could not. "I felt like as a mother something inside me rose up," she recalls. "Ari was just a teenager going to yeshiva every day. He was a good brother, a good son, a good student... he was my child and I will fight for him to my dying day."

Devorah refused to stop fighting until officials investigated the crime as something more serious and insidious than a simple homicide. She realized that Rashid was part of a cell operating out of his local Brooklyn mosque and he'd set out that day to murder.

"Rashid Baz was looking for Jews," Devorah said. "Ari was a *Kadosh* (a holy martyr) and he represented every Jew in the world." She wouldn't rest until his murder was properly investigated by the US federal government as an act of terrorism.

Devorah spent years calling for a re-examination of the case, cornering senators and congressmen and traveling back and forth to Washington. In the process, Devorah transformed herself into an expert on law enforcement and counter-terrorism. "I was like everybody else in the *frum* (religious Jewish) community," Devorah explained. "I knew nothing about the criminal justice system, I knew nothing about guns." She immersed herself in this alien world, and became a respected authority on crime.

In 1998, Devorah sued the Cobray Gun Company, which manufactured one of the guns Baz used to murder her son, as well as six other companies which manufactured gun parts used in the shooting. She lost that lawsuit, but was undaunted and pursued stricter gun control and anti-terrorism laws.

Devorah worked with New York Governor George Pataki, helping to write the first laws on terrorism in New York's penal code: they were signed into law the week of the September 11, 2001 terror attacks. "They were already used in two cases," she noted in a 2021 interview, helping send convicted terrorists to jail. Devorah also helped write "Ari's Law," a New York law which prohibits interstate gun trafficking. She maintains a punishing schedule of legal work, political advocacy, and public speaking.

"If I had to use one word to describe Devorah," recalled former New York Police Department Commissioner Raymond Kelly, "I would use the word relentless. She's a major force in the political world, and certainly those people who focus on the issues of counterterrorism know that well."

After years of painstaking research, Devorah realized that Ari's murder, far from being a spur-of-the-moment crime, as Rahid Baz's lawyer had argued at his trial, was a planned act of terror. In the 1990's, it wasn't yet as evident as it is today that radical Islamism was a global threat. Yet Devorah learned that Baz had been influenced by a radical Islamist ideology and had heard hateful sermons in his Brooklyn mosque. At the time of Ari's murder, Baz had acquired guns and had "military style" weapons in his vehicle.

In 1999, the FBI reopened the case, and in 2000 they declared Ari's murder to be an act of terrorism. That same year, New York's then-Governor George Pataki appointed Devorah to the state's first Commission on Terrorism. Devorah's message that crimes that are motivated by political ideology deserve a different approach from law enforcement was finally gaining traction. The following year, after the attacks of September 11, 2001, it finally became clear to the rest of the world just how dangerous radical Islamism can be.

Busy with a rigorous schedule of addressing and educating law enforcement officials and lawmakers, Devorah also found time to realize another ambition in the wake of Ari's tragic murder: the establishment of the Jewish Children's Museum in Brooklyn, which she co-founded and for which she serves as Director of External Affairs. Opened since 2005, the museum is dedicated to the memory of Ari Halberstam, z"l (*zichrona l'brocha* - of blessed memory). Devorah explains that "the Museum is a setting for children of all faiths and backgrounds to learn about Judaism, and ensures that more people have an understanding of Jewish culture and history."

It's a way of making sure that more people have an understanding Jews and the Jewish community as a method of fighting anti-Semitism, and hatred and bigotry in general. "My belief is building bridges and education. That's what the museum is all about." Public schools bring groups of children to the museum, allowing kids to learn more about Jews. Devorah has seen the positive impact of these visits on kids' attitudes firsthand.

"Kids...are born innocent, they're not born with hate," Devorah observes. After visiting the Jewish museum, she has seen countless children who "have walked out different than how they walked in," with more tolerance and warm feelings towards Jews and others who are different from themselves.

As the Chairwoman of the NYPD Hate Crime Review Panel, Devorah once again worked to make a difference. In cases where it's difficult to determine whether a crime was motivated by hate, the panel reviews evidence, making recommendations which can aid prosecutors as they build their case.

Devorah's tragic experiences and pain motivate her to fight for victims of hate crimes. Asked how she found the courage and motivation to go on after Ari's murder, Devorah explains "I'm a religious Jew... *Ani ma'amin* (I believe). God has a big plan, and whatever happens occurs for a reason."

In all her work, Devorah draws on her deep reserves of faith and strength.

"There's nothing I can do to bring Ari back," she explains. But by recognizing terrorism and hate for what they are, Devorah is trying to spare other people the grief and pain she's gone through. "The lesson doesn't belong to me personally. Ari is each and every one of our children. He's your child..."

Kol Yisrael arevim zeh b'zeh, Devorah notes, echoing the Jewish saying, "All Jews are responsible for one another" (Talmud Shevuot 39a). "It's our job to give to each other, to protect each other, and to stand up for each other." Today, with the Jewish community buffeted by rising hate, this lesson is more important than ever.

Genie Milgrom
born 1958

Genie Milgrom always knew her family was a little different. Born in Cuba into an upper-class Catholic family, she could trace her ancestors' history back hundreds of years to a small town in Spain. When Genie was a young child, the Communist revolution swept Cuba and Genie's family fled the island in 1960, settling in a vibrant Cuban refugee neighborhood in Miami.

Though her family couldn't take all of their possessions with them, they were careful to bring several boxes of family documents. Some of these papers were hundreds of years old and her family had always prided themselves on keeping track of their family tree and unique family customs: no matter where they'd moved in the years since they left Spain, they were always careful to cart several boxes of papers with them.

Genie recalled that even though her Catholic Cuban community was very tight-knit, she always felt her family was different. "I was very close with my mother's mother and used to love cooking and baking with her when I was a child." Her grandmother had a few unique customs. Whenever they would bake bread, they would tear off a small piece of dough, wrap it in foil, and put it in the back of the oven to burn. Whenever a recipe required eggs, Genie and her grandmother would crack them and first check for blood spots, discarding eggs that weren't clear.

When they washed lettuce and other vegetables, they would first check them carefully for bugs using a bright light.

"All these things were being taught to me when I was a child," Genie explains: she assumed that some customs, like burning a portion of dough, were for good luck. Yet they seemed more important to her grandmother than just a good luck charm. Even when her grandmother was elderly and frail, she would still make an effort to get up and check that Genie had separated and burned a piece of dough. If Genie forgot, her grandmother insisted that she go back and do so.

Another strange family custom was only marrying relatives. Going back hundreds of years, family members would only marry other members of their large extended family. Genie's mother was the very first descendant to break with this tradition, marrying Genie's father from outside the clan. Another curious practice that only recently began to be discarded was not eating pork, even though pork and ham were popular foods among both Spanish and Cuban families. For Genie's family the food was taboo.

When Genie married her first husband, a man from the Catholic Cuban community, she learned about another family custom: "Before the ceremony, my mother and grandmother rushed up and pinned shawls to our backs." The shawls were reminiscent, she now feels, of tallises, or Jewish prayer shawls.

Genie and her first husband had two children together, but she always felt something wasn't quite right: "By the time I was 28, I was ready to question my Catholic upbringing." Her marriage unraveled, and Genie started working for her family's global medical supply business, traveling around the world selling health care items.

Spending hours on long flights, Genie read voraciously. "I started to examine what was happening in my soul," she explains. She learned about Jewish life, then later visited Miami-area synagogues to see what Judaism looked like in practice. She longed to see what life was like in an Orthodox synagogue, where all of the Jewish laws and traditions she'd read so much about were practiced. One day, she made the trek to the only Orthodox synagogue near her home, Young Israel of Kendall in Miami, a small congregation. Genie will never forget walking into the building for the first time. "I wound up in a little *shteibel*," she recalled, using the Yiddish word for a small synagogue, "and this is where I said, 'Oh my gosh, I'm home'."

Genie spoke with the rabbi and explained her attraction to Judaism and her desire to convert. To her great surprise, the rabbi listened to her intently but told her that he couldn't help her. Judaism discourages proselytizing and it took more than one meeting with the rabbi for Genie to convince him she was serious about becoming Jewish. Eventually, she met with the local Beit Din (rabbinic court) in Miami, and began the long, slow process of conversion.

It took about five years and it wasn't always easy. Genie taught herself Hebrew and continued to read. Her family wasn't enthusiastic about her journey and there were times when she felt very much alone. Eventually, Genie made one good friend at shul – a woman named Bonnie – who helped and encouraged her. It was Bonnie who went with Genie when she was finally ready to convert. The moment she emerged from the mikveh (ritual bath) after her conversion was an intense spiritual experience. "This was the moment of my greatest accomplishment."

Genie's family didn't share her enthusiasm for her new Jewish life. Her grandmother, in particular, seemed distraught. "She was visibly upset when I converted," Genie said, "and kept telling me it was dangerous to be a Jew." Genie assumed that as a Catholic, her grandmother feared that becoming Jewish posed a spiritual danger. But her unease seemed to be so extreme, Genie suspected that her grandmother harbored an unspoken fear about being a Jew. Sadly, Genie never had the chance to discuss with her the root cause of her fears.

Genie observed Shabbat and kosher laws, and got involved with her synagogue, yet life wasn't always easy for a working single mother. On a business trip to Santiago, Genie met Michael Milgrom, a religious Jew whose family came from Romania and Russia. Michael's upbringing could not have been more different from Genie's: he'd attended some of the world's most prestigious yeshivas in New York and Jerusalem, and was part of a large Orthodox family. They soon recognized that they were soul mates. Genie and Michael married and Michael's family welcomed her with open arms. Genie was now part of the warm Jewish family she'd always wanted.

The couple moved into a new home in Miami and Genie became the president of the sisterhood and the treasurer of the shul. Then her beloved grandmother passed away, on a Friday morning. "Shabbat was fast approaching," Genie said, "and I assumed that she would be buried on the following Sunday or Monday, as was customary in the Catholic faith. But my mother told me that our family tradition was to bury people very soon after their deaths, the same day if possible." Genie was shocked to hear that they were following this Jewish custom and protested that as an Orthodox Jew she would be unable to attend a funeral on Shabbat. But Genie's mother was adamant and she followed family tradition, burying Genie's grandmother the next day, Saturday.

It was a terrible time. Though friends stopped by to be with her, she felt awful that she missed her grandmother's funeral. Later in the afternoon, Genie's mother drove up and made an unannounced visit, handing Genie a small box. "Your grandmother wanted you to have this the day she died," Genie's mother said, then left, still miffed about Genie's actions.

Genie took the box inside and opened it. Inside were two pieces of very old, worn jewelry. One was a small old hamsa charm and the other a tiny gold earring with a Jewish Star of David inside. The pieces finally clicked and Genie had the shocking realization that many of her seemingly quirky family customs were actually Jewish in origin. Separating and burning a piece of dough when one makes bread is a mitzvah, a commandment, that Jewish women around the world perform with a blessing when making a significant amount of dough. Checking for blood in eggs and for insects on vegetables are also both Jewish laws in preparing food, ensuring that we don't violate the Torah's prohibitions on eating blood or insects. Marrying cousins would have ensured that Genie's family remained Jewish, with only Jews marrying other Jews.

"When I saw my grandmother's Jewish jewelry, I fell back on my chair and realized that from beyond the grave Grandma was telling me we're Jewish."

Genie's mother brushed off her inquiries. Perhaps a Gypsy had given the jewelry to the family, she said. Finally her mother gave Genie some old family papers they'd carried with them through the generations. Among the documents Genie found a family tree going back hundreds of years, to 1750. Genie started doing genealogical research and found an online community of people who, like her, suspected that their families might be descended from secret Jews from Spain who'd stayed behind after Jews were formally expelled from Spain in 1492. "I was certain we were from Crypto-Jews who were forced to hide their Jewishness from the Inquisition. Since I was so happy being Jewish, I wanted to sing it from the rooftops, and wanted my kids to know the joy of being Jewish too," Genie explains.

Genie decided to hire a professional genealogist to help. Knowing that Jewish lineage goes through the mother, Genie asked him only to trace her family tree through her maternal line. If she could prove that her maternal ancestors were Jewish, then her grandmother, her mother, she and other relatives were Jewish from birth as well. "I told the genealogist just follow the maternal grandmothers back until you find they're Jews."

The genealogist didn't mince words. ""You're nuts!' he said." Tracing a family back so many generations – over 500 years to a time when Jews could live openly in Spain before 1492 – seemed impossible. Yet Genie was undeterred. "There were two options: either I was nuts or I was right. And I wanted to be right." The strong feelings she'd always had drawing her to Judaism gave Genie hope. "I had this feeling that I was Jewish from birth and I wanted desperately to prove that."

It took eight years, but the genealogist found documents tracing Genie's family line back to 1545 in Spain. Before that, Church records weren't as well organized and research was much more difficult. Genie was able to trace her family back to a small town called Fermoselle in western Spain, and by then she'd identified 800 ancestors. She and Michael decided to travel to Fermoselle in Spain and see what they could find.

They visited the town with other researchers, and after much work and many conversations with local historians, they made some startling discoveries. The Spanish Inquisition lasted from 1478 to 1834 and had broad powers to root out any supposed Catholic who seemed to be performing Jewish rites in secret. Anyone found to be practicing Judaism or even suspected could be burnt to death. Yet some secret Jews did succeed in leaving messages for each other. Genie found some intriguing carvings on Fermoselle's church and other buildings. One carving shows a large cross with a sword going across it. Atop the cross is a Jewish menorah and on the bottom are twelve balls. Could these represent the twelve Jewish Tribes, under the nose of the Catholic Church? The carving was topped with the Hebrew letters *yud, hey, vov* and *hey*, spelling out the Hebrew word for God.

Eventually Genie and other researchers uncovered the ruins of a synagogue and what appeared to be two ancient mikvehs in Fermoselle. An elderly resident even whispered to them that she'd heard there had once been a Jewish quarter in the town. Some of the houses were connected to one another via underground secret tunnels; perhaps these enabled secret Jews to flee from Inquisition authorities.

Most chilling for Genie was a story that locals told her about a field outside of town that was called *El Humilladero*, or "The Humiliation." Animals used to be slaughtered there, locals explained. For years there was a curious custom: residents of some towns across the River Duero that flowed near Fermoselle and divided Spain from Portugal used to make an annual pilgrimage to the empty field. There, they would leave stones, echoing the Jewish custom of placing stones on top of graves. When she heard this, Genie felt certain that *El Humilladero* was where Jews were once humiliated and publicly burned by the Inquisition, and that the pilgrims laying stones were secret Jews honoring their memories. Genie made her way to the field and recited *Kaddish*, the Jewish prayer for the dead.

Gazing across the Duero River into Portugal, Genie suddenly had an idea. Portugal had its own Inquisition, but it didn't start until 1536, years after Spain's Inquisition started hunting for secret Jews. What if her ancestors had simply crossed the river into Portugal to find religious freedom? Genie put the idea to the genealogist she hired. He began looking at nearby villages in Portugal. Genie's hunch was right: within a day her genealogist found 45 relatives he could prove were directly related to her family. After consulting with yet more researchers, Genie finally had proof she was related to people who'd once lived openly as Jews.

While conducting this in-depth, groundbreaking research, Genie read the original Inquisition records and was horrified at the tortures inflicted on her ancestors and other secret Jews in Spain. "I finally understood why there was such a strong feeling inside of me," she said. "These grandmothers were killed for not eating pork, for changing sheets on Friday, for not cleaning house on Shabbat. These women were burned at the stake for things I do every day."

It took fifteen years of painstaking research, but Genie finally had proof that her maternal line – and other branches of her family as well – had once lived openly as Jews. She had long been in touch with a rabbinical court in Jerusalem that has the power to grant conversions, and she packed copies of every document in a box and shipped it to them. "I eventually got a letter from the Beit Din Gadol saying God brought me to this place, that there should never ever again be a question that I was born Jewish, and that all descendants from me are Jews."

Genie has written six books and shared her experiences with many other people who felt they might be descended from secret Jews. "I'm not doing this for me anymore," she explains. Genie also has a message for her fellow Jews who may take being Jewish for granted. "My story resonates with Jews from all backgrounds because here is a person who was literally crying for something that other people just toss by the wayside. I want Jews to appreciate the treasure they have in being Jewish."

Fifteen generations separate Genie from her relatives who last lived openly as Jews. These fifteen grandmothers could never assert their Jewishness while they were alive, but now Genie is determined to remember them and honor their lives.

Genie lights two extra Shabbat candles in honor of the many grandmothers she uncovered who were born Jewish but were never able to light Shabbat candles of their own. When she lights them, Genie pictures them standing beside her, sharing this holy moment with their great, great, great grand-daughter Genie.

After years of painstaking research she's uncovered the names of grandmothers: Ascension Diez Flores; Maria Basilia Flores Alvarez; Maria Manuela Alvarez Garrido; Teresa Garrido Mayor; Jacinta Mayor Martin; Josefa Martin Fincia Montano; Anna Maria Funcia Montano Fernando o Fernandez(s); Teresa Fernando Rodrigues(z) o Fernandez(s); Maria Rodriguez Montano; Catalina Guerra Rodriguez; Catalina Rodriguez(s) Ramirez; Maria Rodriguez Santos Goveia; Phelipa Rodriguez; Maria Ramires Rodriguez; Catalina Ramires.

These women represent a straight line going back to pre-Inquisition Spain. And to this list, add Genie Milgrom, a proud Jew who finally found her way home to Jewish life after 500 long years.

Penina Tamano-Shata
Born 1981

When Penina Tamano-Shata was sworn in as Israel's Minister of Aliyah and Integration on May 17, 2020, she became the most senior Ethiopian-born government official Israel ever had. "For me, this is a landmark and the closing of a circle," she explained at the time. "From that three-year old girl who immigrated to Israel without a mother on a cross-desert foot journey, through growing up in Israel and the struggles I led and am still leading for the community, integration, the acceptance of the other, and against discrimination and racism."

Penina was born in 1981: in the chaos of Ethiopia's brutal civil war, her exact birth date was lost; she later chose November 1 as her birthday once she reached Israel. Her family was prominent in their home village of Wuzaba, near the Gondar region in northern Ethiopia, where most of Ethiopia's sizable Jewish community lived for thousands of years, since the time of the First Temple. Her grandfather, Kes Shato, was one of Ethiopian Jews' spiritual leaders.

Ethiopian Jews started fleeing the country when civil war broke out in 1974 and periodic famines swept the country. For four years, Israel was able to broker the top-secret release of Ethiopian Jews in exchange for supplying government forces with weapons. Ethiopia's embattled leaders gradually moved into the Soviet sphere of influence during the war, and when reporters finally uncovered Israel's arms-for-refugees agreement with Ethiopia in 1978, they slammed the doors of Jewish emigration shut. During all of that year, Ethiopia's ruling officials allowed only three Jews to emigrate. Flights to Israel from Ethiopian territory were strictly barred.

Still desperate to leave, Ethiopian Jews found a new, more treacherous route to freedom: thousands of Jewish families began walking across war-torn countryside and scorching desert scrubland into neighboring Sudan, where they huddled in refugee camps, waiting for a way to get to Israel. In 1984, the Tamano family joined this mass exodus. In all, 16,000 Ethiopian Jews made the difficult trek to Sudan. Fully 1,500 died on the way, or perished in the refugee camps in Sudan.

The trip was a monumental challenge for the Tamanos. Penina's mother was heavily pregnant, and unable to walk such long distances; one of Penina's brothers carried her on his back. Another brother carried Penina, who was just three years old. Miraculously, they made it to a refugee camp in Sudan, where Penina's mother had her baby, but there was little food and no adequate medical care. "After she gave birth, she was dying," Penina later told *The Jerusalem Post*; Penina's older sister nursed their mother back to help and took care of the newborn.

"The refugee camp in Sudan was just tents, and we were in a Muslim country in 50 degree (Celsius - 122 Fahrenheit) heat. The people who remember it say people were afraid to go to the Red Cross," Penina's described. "I have friends my age whose parents died there… My husband lost two sisters, who were two and three years old, on the way to Israel. I was privileged to have made it."

In 1984, Israel's government devised a plan to rescue Ethiopian Jews who'd made it to Sudan. Dubbed Operation Moses, it commenced on November 21, 1984. Over the course of six weeks, over 30 flights flew nearly 8,000 Jews from Sudan to Brussels, then on to Israel. Operation Moses came to an abrupt end when details leaded out on January 5, 1985. A thousand Jews remained in Sudan for another year, until a second airlift, dubbed Operation Sheba, brought most of them to Israel.

196

Penina's family was torn apart in the chaos of the rescue. She, her father, and her five brothers boarded a truck to take them from the refugee camp to the airstrip, while her mother, the new baby, and Penina's sister rode in another truck. Penina's group made it to the airplane - but the truck her mother and sister were on broke down. Three-year old Penina flew to Israel with her father and brothers, leaving the rest of their family behind. Her mother waited over a year for another airlift when she could finally join her family in Israel. It was a traumatic time.

Her family moved into an absorption center in the north of Israel. "I'm very open, I like people," she reminisced about her first weeks in Israel. "When we lived in the absorption center, my sisters were six and eight and I was three. Whenever we'd go outside and walk around, I would say hello to everyone, to every white person. We came from a small village where everyone always greeted everyone, but my sisters would stop me and tell me we don't do that here."

In a sense, though, Penina never did stop greeting and connecting with everyone she met. Her family moved to Petah Tikva, where Penina lives today with her husband Zion and their two children. Penina went to religious schools, including a stint in boarding school. She grew up fast: "When I was seven, I switched to 'adult mode,'" she recalled, "I was my parents' voice, standing up for their rights when people would cut in line or disrespect them." Penina began working menial jobs after school at age eleven.

Despite her family's struggles, Penina never lost her sense of wonder at living in Israel. "Our dream came true," Penina has explained; "it was a dream with challenges, that separated families, but I was so lucky, and my family was reunited. Anyone who has made aliyah, even at a very young age, (it) shapes your character for life... I felt Israel the moment my foot touched this country."

As Minister, Penina reflected: "Looking back, I think it just made me stronger - being part of the low class, witnessing discrimination. I learned early on to fight for my own rights."

She was a brilliant student, and a high school program for gifted teens broadened her horizons. After serving in Israel's army, Penina earned a law degree and served as president of the Ethiopian Student Association. Her first job was being a reporter with Israel's popular Channel 1. She later anchored a current affairs show with Uri Levy, who recalled "We immediately realized (Penina) had immense talent, knowledge and analytical abilities. I've always known she'd make it to politics. Penina is a person with great social awareness and a will to make a difference."

Though she excelled in journalism, Penina wanted to be an agent of change, not a reporter covering other people's actions. When Channel 1 asked her to cover a large protest against discrimination, instead of taking the assignment, she asked for the day off - and joined the protest: "When you work for the media you have to remain objective, and I often wanted to take an active part."

She quit journalism and ran for Israel's Knesset with the Yesh Atid party. Penina won her first election, serving in the Knesset from 2013 to 2015, then from 2019 to 2020, when incoming Deputy Prime Minister Benny Gantz invited her to join Israel's new government as Minister for Aliyah and Integration. It was a symbolic moment, laden with emotion. "Benny was there in the desert for Operation Moses," Penina told journalists at the time, referring to Gantz's illustrious military record, which included time in Ethiopia and Sudan helping with the airlifts. "He saw it. He may have even seen me. He saw the children and knows exactly what we went through… It was an honor to get this appointment from him."

In office, Penina has had to cope with some of Israel's greatest challenges. When the Covid-19 pandemic shut down much of Israeli society, Penina insisted that the route to Aliyah remain open so that Jews could continue immigrating to the Jewish state. "From the time of the establishment of the country, we have never stopped Aliyah: 'We cannot do this,' I said, and I was the only one to vote against (closing Israel's airport), and I'm proud of it," she declared at the time. With most commercial routes closed during the worst days of the pandemic, Penina arranged charter flights so that new citizens could arrive in Israel.

She campaigned to exempt immigrants from Israel's Covid-era ban on people over the age of 70 arriving in the country, and encouraged businesses hard-hit by lockdowns to hire new immigrants by paying half their salaries. Penina also ensured that children of new immigrants could attend the few Israeli schools that remained open during the pandemic: "How could they study with Zoom if they don't have the language, if they don't have friends?" she asked.

As Minister, she expanded Israel's allowance of subsidized Hebrew classes offered to new immigrants from two and a half years to ten, and was an advocate for facilitating conversion for people who've immigrated to Israel under the Law of Return, which allows anyone with one Jewish parent or grandparent to apply for citizenship. Penina is outspoken about the way she identifies with each new immigrant her office helps settle in the Jewish state. "I'm just Penina," she told reporters when she was first appointed Minister and was unused to the trappings of her office: "The girl who arrived in Israel barefoot is still me."

When war erupted in Ukraine following Russia's invasion in March 2022, Penina lobbied to ease immigration requirements for Ukrainian refugees, even threatening to quit if more wasn't done to help. "Our message to the Jews of Ukraine is clear," she declared. "Israel will always be your home; our gates are open to you in normal times and also in times of emergency....and we are ready to absorb thousands of immigrants - anyone who wants to come to Israel."

As Israel's first Ethiopian-born Minister, Penina is used to representing her community and has long advocated for better treatment for Israel's 140,000 strong Ethiopian population. She is aware of her role as a symbol for Ethiopian Jews in Israel. "I have so many identities," she's said: "Jewish, woman, Black, but my first identity is Jewish - you can't not say that being a Black woman influenced me, but my home is the Jewish heart."

Recommended for Further Reading

American Jewish Women's History: A Reader, Edited by Pamela S. Nadell. (New York University Press, New York: 2003).

Eliyahu's Branches: The Descendants of the Vilna Gaon (of Blessed and Saintly Memory) and his Family by Chaim Freedman. (Avotaynu: 1997).

Expulsion: England's Jewish Solution: The Story of How England's Kings First Courted Then Persecuted and Finally Expelled England's Jewish Community During the Middle Ages by Richard Huscroft. (Tempus Publishing Ltd., Stroud, Gloucestershire: 2006).

Dona Gracia of the House of Nasi by Cecil Roth (1946).

The Golden Tradition: Jewish Life and Thought in Eastern Europe by Lucy S. Dawidowicz. (Holt, Rinehart and Winston, New York: 1967).

Hannah Senesh: Her Life and Diary. Forward by Margy Piercy. Preface by Eitan Senesh. (Jewish Lights Publishing, Woodstock, VT: 2007).

Heroes of Israel: Profiles of Jewish Courage by Chaim Herzog. (Little, Brown and Co, Boston: 1989).

HIdden Heroes: One Woman's Story of Resistance and Rescue in the Soviet Union by Pamela Braun Cohen. (Gefen Publishing House, Jerusalem: 2021).

In Kindling Flame: The Story of Hannah Senesh 1921-1944 by Linda Atkinson. (Lothrop, Lee & Shepard Books, New York: 1985).

A Jewish Woman's Prayer Book, Edited by Aliza Lavie. (Spiegel & Grau, New York: 2008).

The Jew in the Medieval World: A Source Book: 315-1791 by Jacob Rader Marcus. (Hebrew Union College Press, Cincinnati: 1999).

The Jews of Kurdistan by Erich Brauer, completed and edited by Raphael Patai. (Wayne State University Press, Detroit: 1993).

Judaism in Practice: From the Middle Ages Through the Early Modern Period edited by Lawrence Fine. (Princeton Readings in Religions, Princeton University Press, Princeton, New Jersey: 2001).

Lawrence in Arabia: War, Deceit, Imperial Folly and the Making of the Modern Middle East by Scott Anderson. (Doubleday Books, New York: 2013).

Licoricia of Winchester: Marriage, Motherhood and Murder by Suzanne Bartlett. (Valentine Mitchell Publishers, London: 2015).

The Light of Days: The Untold Story of Women Resistance Fighters in Hitler's Ghettos by Judy Batalion. (William Morrow, New York: 2020).

The Maiden of Ludomir: A Jewish Holy Woman and Her World by Nathaniel Deutsch. (University of California Press, Berkeley, CA: 2009).

The Martyrdom of a Moroccan Jewish Saint by Sharon Vance. Brill's Series in Jewish Studies. Volume 44. Edited by David S. Katz. (Brill, Leiden, Boston: 2011).

Medieval Jewish Civilization: An Encyclopedia, edited by Norman Roth. (Routledge, New York: 2003).

The Memoirs of Gluckel of Hameln, Translated by Marvin Lowenthal with an Introduction by Robert Rosen. (Schocken Books, New York: 1977).

Men of Silk: The Hasidic Conquest of Polish Jewish Society by Glenn Dynner. (Oxford University Press, Oxford: 2006).

Meneket Rivkah: A Manual of Wisdom and Piety for Jewish Women by Rivke Bat Meir, Introduction and Commentary by Frauke Von Rohden. Translation by Samuel Spinner. Translation of Introduction and Commentary by Maurice Tszorf. (Jewish Publication Society, Philadelphia: 2009).

My Fifteen Grandmothers by Genie Milgrom. (CreateSpace Independent Publishing Platform: 2012).

My Life by Golda Meir. (G.P. Putnam's Sons, New York: 1975).

My Life and Experiences at "Shaare Zedek" by Shvester Selma (Published in 1973 and 2001 by Shaare Tzedek, Jerusalem).

Nehama Leibowitz: Teacher and Bible Scholar by Yael Unterman. (Urim Publications, Brooklyn, New York: 2009).

New Studies in Bamidbar / Numbers by Nehama Leibowitz. Translated and adapted from the Hebrew by Aryeh Newman. Fourth Edition. (World Zionist Organization, Jerusalem: 1981.)

New Studies in Bereshit / Genesis by Nehama Leibowitz. Translated and adapted from the Hebrew by Aryeh Newman. Fourth Edition. (World Zionist Organization, Jerusalem: 1981.)

New Studies in Devarim / Deuteronomy by Nehama Leibowitz. Translated and adapted from the Hebrew by Aryeh Newman. Fourth Edition. (World Zionist Organization, Jerusalem: 1981.)

New Studies in Shemot / Exodus by Nehama Leibowitz. Translated and adapted from the Hebrew by Aryeh Newman. Fourth Edition. (World Zionist Organization, Jerusalem: 1981.)

New Studies in Vayikra / Leviticus by Nehama Leibowitz. Translated and adapted from the Hebrew by Aryeh Newman. Fourth Edition. (World Zionist Organization, Jerusalem: 1981.)

Notes from a Private Journal of a Visit to Egypt and Palestine, by Way of Italy and the Mediterranean by Judith Montefiore. (Printed by Palala Press: 2015).

Operation Solomon: The Daring Rescue of the Ethiopian Jews by Stephen Spector. (Oxford University Press: 2005).

Pious and Rebellious: Jewish Women in Medieval Europe by Avraham Grossman. Translated from the Hebrew by Jonathan Chipman. (Brandeis University Press, Waltham, Massachusetts: 2004).

Power of the Weak: Studies on Medieval Women edited by Jennifer Carpenter and Sally-Beth MacLean (1995).

The Sassoons: The Great Global Merchants and the Making of an Empire by Joseph Sassoon. (Pantheon Books, New York: 2022)

The Prime Ministers: An Intimate Narrative of Israeli Leadership by Yehuda Avner. (The Toby Press, LLC, New Milford, CT: 2012).

"Rabbi Asnat: A Female Yeshiva Director in Kurdistan," by Uri Melammed and Renee Levine, *Pe'amim* 82 (2000): 163-178.

Rebbetzin Grunfeld: The Life of Judith Grunfeld, Courageous Pioneer of the Bais Yaakov Movement and Jewish Rebirth by Miriam Dansky. (Mesorah Publications, Ltd., Brooklyn, NY: 1994).

Rebecca Gratz: Women and Judaism in Antebellum America by Dianne Ashton. (Wayne State University Press, Detroit: 1997).

Sarah Schenirer and the Bais Yaakov Movement: A Revolution in the Name of Tradition by Naomi Seidman. (The Littman Library of Jewish Civilization, London: 2019).

Seyder Tkhines: The Forgotten Book of Common Prayer for Jewish Women by Devra Kay. (The Jewish Publication Society, Philadelphia: 2004).

Spies in Palestine: Love, Betrayal, and the Heroic Life of Sarah Aaronsohn by James Srodes. (Counterpoint, Berkeley: 2016).

Tales of Nehama: Impressions of the Life and Teachings of Nehama Leibowitz by Leah Abramowitz. (Gefen Publishing House, Ltd., Jerusalem: 2003).

To Repair a Broken World: The Life of Henrietta Szold, Founder of Hadassah by Dvora Hacohen. (Harvard University Press: 2021).

Tosia Altman: From the Leadership of Ha-Shomer ha-Zai'ir to the Command of the ZOB (Hebrew), by Ziva Shalev. (Tel Aviv, 1992).

The Woman Who Defied Kings: The Life and Times of Dona Gracia Nasi by Andree Aelion Brooks (2002).

The Women of Rothschild: The Untold Story of the World's Most Famous Dynasty by Natalie Livingstone. (John Murray: 2021).

X Troop: The Secret Jewish Commandos of World War II by Leah Garrett. (Houghton Mifflin Harcourt, Boston: 2021).

Discussion Questions

1. Which of the women in this book did you most identify with? Why?

2. Which women profiled in this book did you like the most? Who did you like the least? Do you think it's possible to learn from role models one doesn't much like? Why or why not?

3. Many of the women in this book transgressed gender norms. Do you feel they were motivated by feminism or by other rationales?

4. Some of the women in this book engaged in money lending, a profession that has long been regarded negatively. Did reading about their lives change your feelings about money lending? Did reading about Jewish money lenders make you feel uncomfortable? Why or why not?

5. The title of this book, *Portraits of Valor*, implies that the women profiled here were heroic. Do you agree? Do you feel they all belong in this book? Are some more worthy of admiration than others?

6. If you could choose one woman in this book to invite over for dinner, who would it be? What would you like to say to her?

7. Sarah Aaronsohn asked that her "blood be avenged" after her death. She, like many of the women in this book, died in the course of her struggle to live a Jewish life or to promote Jewish self determination. Do you think other women in this book would want their "blood (to) be avenged?" Do you agree with that sentiment? What responsibility, if any, do you feel for honoring the memories of the women in this book who were killed for being Jewish?

8. Which of the women in this book would you like to learn more about? What aspects of their lives would you like to know more about? How do you intend to learn more about them?

9. Do you think it makes sense to read a book about Jewish women? Did you feel that the women profiled in this book shared common characteristics due to their gender? Would you have preferred to read about Jewish heroes, both male and female, instead, or about women in general? Why or why not?

10. Have any of the women in this book inspired you to do something different in your own life? Please describe what that is and why her example motivates you.